AUTHOR

Since 2009, Chris Flaherty has written for the UK Armourer Magazine; Classic Arms & Militaria; and, Soldiers of the Queen Journal. He has advised major international museums on uniforms. For Partizan Press in 2014, he wrote and illustrated two books: 'Turkish Uniforms of the Crimean War: A Handbook of Uniforms'; and, 'The Ottoman Army in the First World War: A Handbook of Uniforms'. He co-authored and illustrated with Bruno Mugnai for Soldiershop Publishing: 2014 'Der Lange Turkenkrieg (1593-1606), Volume 1: The Long Turkish – War Habsburg Arrests the Ottoman Advance; and, in 2015 'Der Lange Turkenkrieg (1593- 1606), Volume 2: The Long Turkish War'. In 2015, he was a contributor (illustrator) to the Turkish Gallipoli Centenary Exhibition: 'From Depths to the Trenches: Gallipoli 1915', at the Isbank Museum in Istanbul. He was one of the contributors to, 'Philip Jowett, 2015 Armies of the Greek-Turkish War 1919–22', Men-at-Arms 50, Osprey Publishing. He authored a chapter on the, 'Ottoman Army in the Great Northern War' appearing in Stephen, L. Kling, Jr. (Editor) 2016 GNW Compendium: A Collection of Articles on the Great Northern War, 1700-1721 (Volume 2), The Historical Game Company. He has authored and illustrated for Partizan Press' Universal Wargames Rules Supplements: 'Napoleonic Small Siege, River Ship, Gunboat and Pontooning' (2016); 'Napoleonic Foraging, Insurrection, Marauders, Bakeries, Convoy and Encampment Wargaming' (2016); 'Napoleonic Balloon Warfare' (2017); 'Napoleonic Ottoman Army Wargaming Supplement' (2018); 'A Wargamer's Guide to WW1 Ottoman Army Uniforms' (2018); 'Napoleon's July 1798 Pyramid Campaign & the Egyptian Army' (2019); 'The Napoleonic Ottoman Army: Uniforms, Tactics and Organization' (2019). Since 2021 he has written and illustrated several titles for Soldiershop Publishing, including: 'The Sardinian Expeditionary Corps'.

PUBLISHER'S NOTES

None of unpublished images or text of our book may be reproduced in any format without the expressed written permission of Soldiershop.com when not indicate as marked with license creative commons 3.0 or 4.0. Soldiershop Publishing has made every reasonable effort to locate, contact and acknowledge rights holders and to correctly apply terms and conditions to Content. In the event that any Content infringes your rights or the rights of any third parties, or Content is not properly identified or acknowledged we would like to hear from you so we may make any necessary alterations. In this event contact: info@soldiershop.com. Our trademark: Soldiershop Publishing ©, The names of our series & brand: Museum book, Bookmoon, Soldiers&Weapons, Battlefield, War in colour, Historical Biographies, Darwin's view, Fabula, Altrastoria, Italia Storica Ebook, Witness To History, Soldiers, Weapons & Uniforms, Storia etc. are herein © by Soldiershop.com.

LICENSES COMMONS

This book may utilize part of material marked with license creative commons 3.0 or 4.0 (CC BY 4.0), (CC BY-ND 4.0), (CC BY-SA 4.0) or (CC0 1.0). Or derived from publication 70 years old or more and recolored from us. We give appropriate attribution credit and indicate if change were made in the acknowledgements field.
All our books utilize only fonts licensed under the SIL Open Font License or other free use license.

ISBN: 9791255892113   1st edition February 2025
S&W-055 - TURKISH & EGYPTIAN CAVALRY 1879-1922
Written and illustrated by Chris Flaherty
Editor: Luca Cristini Editore, for the brand: Soldiershop. Cover & Art Design: Luca S. Cristini.

CHRIS FLAHERTY

TURKISH & EGYPTIAN CAVALRY 1879-1922

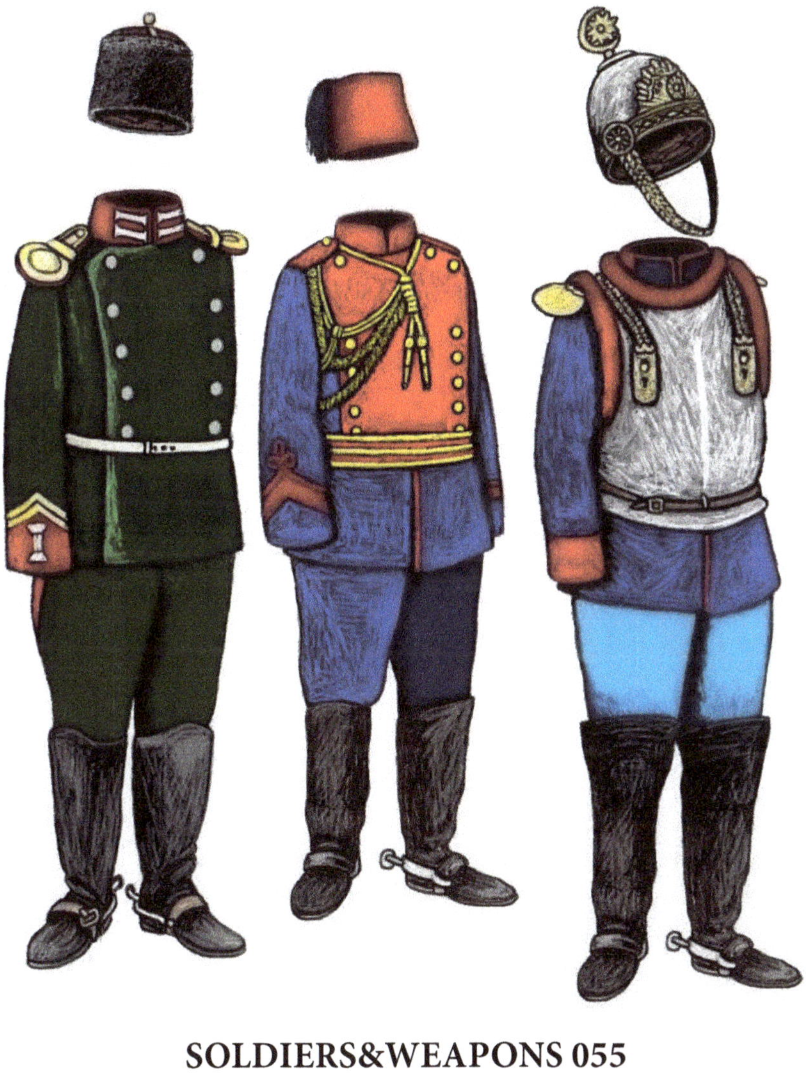

SOLDIERS&WEAPONS 055

CONTENTS & INTRODUCTION

The Turkish Imperial Army under Sultan Abdulhamid, otherwise commonly known as Abdul Hamid II, from 1876 to 1909, saw introduction of a set of standardized and regulated uniforms and insignia. The new suit had a tailored tunic and breeches designed for use by the entire Army. It replaced the 1861 era Zouave uniform. This occurred, "in 1879 in the wake of the Russo-Turkish War"[1]. Marking a return to the tunic, worn by much of the Army in the Crimean War era. From 1879, the Turkish Cavalry consisted of its Dragoon and Lancer, Hamidiye: Irregular Militias, and Mounted Gendarme Regiments. This volume then looks at Turkish Imperial, and later Nationalist Army Cavalry uniforms during the First World War, and Greek-Turkish War. The Egyptian Cavalry divides into two main periods, before and after 1883 (when the new Egyptian Army was formally raised). Before 1883, there was the Line Cavalry and Khedive's Zirkhagi: Iron Men (Cuirassiers). After 1883, several Lancers Troops (Squadrons), and a Khedive's Bodyguard Squadron of Lancers were formed, along with a Camel Corps. Following changes in the British Army over the same period, the Egyptian Army after 1885 saw introduction of the field service khaki uniform, in addition to its traditional summer and winter dress, which was relegated to Barracks wear.

Chapter 1: Turkish Cavalry Organization and Uniforms.................5
Chapter 2: Officer's Rank Insignia.................13
Chapter 3: Imperial Guard Cavalry.................19
Chapter 4: Dragoons and Cuirassiers.................29
Chapter 5: Line Dragoon Cavalry After 1909.................32
Chapter 6: Hejaz Division Cavalry.................35
Chapter 7: Hamidiye Corps.................40
Chapter 8: Mounted Gendarme.................46
Chapter 9: Cavalry Artillery.................53
Chapter 10: Sultan's Standard and Cavalry Sanjakdar.................57
Chapter 11: Egyptian Cavalry.................63
Chapter 12: Egyptian Army Camel Corps.................74
Chapter 13: First World War and Nationalist Army Cavalry.................77
Chapter 14: Camel Raiders.................80
Chapter 15: Cavalry Equipment.................82
References.................90

---

1   Roubicek, 1978.

CHAPTER 1: TURKISH CAVALRY ORGANIZATION AND UNIFORMS

Up till 1878, the Cavalry, like the Infantry retained their territorial titles, when a new system of consecutive numbers was introduced. By the start of the Russo-Turkish War, the Imperial Army had 186 Cavalry Squadrons[1]. This number included some 50 Volunteer Cavalry (Circassians, Arabs, Kurds) Squadrons. While after 1879,

> "[a] … new military organisation was adopted: A Cavalry Division of three Brigades (one attached to the Active Army and two to the Reserves) existed in each of the first five Military Regions. A Brigade comprised two Regiments of Cavalry of five Squadrons each."[2]

By 1898, the Nizam: Regulars were organized into Dragoon and Lancer Cavalry, fielding:

> "39 Standing Regiments of 5 Squadrons each and 2 Half-Regiments of 2 Squadrons each, one Regiment of Remounts, the Sultan Escort Squadron, 12 Regiments of Redeef … [Reserve] … Cavalry, each of 4 Squadrons, and 67 Hamidiye (Irregular Militias)."[3]

The Cavalry consisted of six Divisions, with one Division allocated to six of the Ordu: Armies[4]. Apart from this, there were two Cavalry Regiments in Tripoli and two Cavalry Companies in both the 7th Ordu: Army, and the Hejaz Division. The newly established Ertugrul Cavalry Regiment was attached to the 1st Division in the capital - Constantinople [Istanbul]. Generally, two Regiments formed a Brigade, and three Brigades a Division[5]. The Ertugrul Cavalry Regiment like most of the 1st Ordu: Army, were also assigned to an Imperial Guard organization.

▼ Cavalry Regiments were numbered from 1 to 33[6]. After 1878, the likely consecutive numbering system identified the following Regiments:

1st ORDU: ARMY	
1st Cavalry Lancer Regiment (Imperial Guard)	4th Cavalry Dragoon Regiment
2nd Cavalry Dragoon Regiment (Imperial Guard)	5th Cavalry Dragoon Regiment (Imperial Guard)
3rd Cavalry Dragoon Regiment	6th Cavalry Dragoon Regiment
2ND ORDU: ARMY	4TH ORDU: ARMY
7th Cavalry Lancer Regiment	19th Cavalry Lancer Regiment
8th Cavalry Dragoon Regiment	20th Cavalry Dragoon Regiment
9th Cavalry Dragoon Regiment	21st Cavalry Dragoon Regiment
10th Cavalry Dragoon Regiment	22nd Cavalry Dragoon Regiment
11th Cavalry Dragoon Regiment	23rd Cavalry Dragoon Regiment
12th Cavalry Dragoon Regiment	24th Cavalry Dragoon Regiment
3RD ORDU: ARMY	5TH ORDU: ARMY
13th Cavalry Lancer Regiment	25th Cavalry Lancer Regiment

1 Roubicek, 1978.
2 Roubicek, 1978.
3 Roubicek, 1978.
4 Askeri Muze, 1986.
5 Roubicek, 1978.
6 British General Staff, 1995.

14th Cavalry Dragoon Regiment	26th Cavalry Dragoon Regiment
15th Cavalry Dragoon Regiment	27th Cavalry Dragoon Regiment
16th Cavalry Dragoon Regiment	28th Cavalry Dragoon Regiment
17th Cavalry Dragoon Regiment	29th Cavalry Dragoon Regiment
18th Cavalry Dragoon Regiment	30th Cavalry Dragoon Regiment
6TH ORDU: ARMY	
31st Cavalry Dragoon Regiment	32nd Cavalry Dragoon Regiment

By 1914, the following 6th, 8th, 9th, 10th, 16th, 17th, 18th, 28th, 30th, and 32nd Regiments had been lost, and the remaining Cavalry consisted of the following Regiments[7]: 1st Regiment of Lancers, 2nd, 3rd, 4th, 5th, 7th, 11th, 12th, 13th, 14th, 15th, 19th, 20th, 21st, 22nd (Hejaz Division), 23rd, 24th, 25th, 26th, 27th, 29th, 31st, and 33rd Dragoons. The total forces represented one Special Guard Squadron (Ertugrul Regiment), and 22 Regiments of five Squadrons; and 22nd (Hejaz Division), that was a two Squadrons Regiment.

UNIFORMS

From 1879, Imperial Army organization and uniform reforms saw introduction of a new suit consisting of a dark blue tunic with a short skirt, that stopped at the top of the wearer's thighs, with eight large (some variations show nine: depending on the wearer's height) gilt metal star and crescent buttons, with plain or rope rims down the front. The Cavalry version of the tunic had a low red collar (the Infantry used blue collars with red piping) with red piping down the tunic front. The collar was fitted with angled dark blue patches (Infantry had red patches). Large gilt metal shoulder scales (Infantry wore square ended dark blue shoulder boards edged in red), were cut with Regimental Ottoman-Turkish numerals. The numbers appeared red, as this was the red fabric underlay showing through.

▲ A 1907 illustration, showing a, "General de Brigade d'Cavalerie (Grande Tenue); Colonel du Regiment de Cavalerie Ertogrul; Chef d'Escadron du 1er Regiment de Cavalerie de La Garde – Regiment de Lanciers; Soldat de Cavalerie."[8]

7   British General Staff, 1995.
8   Sevket, 1907.

The back of the tunic was plain except for two rear waist buttons, used to support the belt. However, it was possible the rear vent was piped red, and three corner pockets with buttons decorated the back flaps of the skirt. The cuffs were round and plain red (the Infantry version was dark blue with a top edged in red, and a square patch displaying two buttons). Light blue riding breeches were worn, that had broad red side stripes[9]. An 1893 photograph shows leather covering for the breeches inside leg[10]. Black knee-high riding boots completed the dress[11]. Longer soft German or Russian styled Cavalry boots covering the knees was also worn. Brown leather boots are also depicted[12], and this may match the use of brown leather equipment, which is also shown as black. It is possible Turkish leather equipment was issued untreated brown and these progressively darkened through polishing and greasing.

Till 1908, most of the Imperial Army did not have any formal headgear issued, using instead the national headdress – the civilian Fez. It was only in the Crimean War era that a military Fez was known, distinguished by a large top button, and chinstraps added for Cavalry use. The 1880s uniform included first use of a lamb wool hat - called the Serpus, or the Kalpak (as it is better known after 1909), for Turkish Dragoons and Artillery of all ranks to replace the standard Government manufactured Fez. Kalpak construction shared many similarities with the Fez, and was likely a covered Fez woven cane frame, with the top in plain red, or bottle-green for the 4th Dragoon Cavalry Regiment. Officer's Kalpak had five silver or gilt (depending on the Regiment's button colour) lines of tape forming a star pattern with a decorative button in the centre. Actual lamb wool was specified, however frequently a simulated wool version is seen made from wool carpet weave. It should be noted that from 1861, the Karapapak Tribal Cavalry (who emigrated from Azerbaijan, in the 1820s) wore the traditional Russian Cossacks' uniform, and are also the likely source for this introduction. Headgear like the Imperial Army's Kalpak had also been established in the Persian Army by 1889.

The only variations to the Cavalry tunic was that worn by the 4th Cavalry Regiment which had bottle-green facings like the Infantry Rifle Battalions. While, the 1st Lancers Regiment wore a dark blue tunic that resembled the German-Bavarian Chevaulegers' tunic over the same period, with red collar, cuffs and piping. It also had white metal buttons, near the shoulders, and six more on either side. The tunic was either made with a red paraderabatte: button-on chest lapels, or this was a separate item that buttoned onto the tunic front. The only other variation was that of the Ertugrul Cavalry Regiment which wore a green German-Bavarian Chevaulegers' tunic.

▶ Introduced with the new suit the star and crescent button was still used in the First World War. The dress uniform tunic button[13].

9	Sevket, 1907.
10	Freres, 1893.
11	Askeri Muze, 1986.
12	Sevket, 1907.
13	Askeri Muze, 1986.

GREATCOATS AND WINTER BASHLIK

The Imperial Army's greatcoat was dark blue, had a double-breasted front, with large gilt buttons. The greatcoat had a deep folded-down collar edged in red for the Cavalry, and bottle-green for the 4th Cavalry Regiment. The piping ran down the front of the opening vent. The coat had deep rolled cuffs. The Officers' greatcoat was provided with red shoulder bords to show rank. It is not clear if the Soldier's greatcoat was fitted with plain red (or bottle-green for the 4th Cavalry) shoulder boards (with Regimental numerals in contrasting yellow), or shoulder scales were fitted. The Officer's coat had deep rolled cuffs edged in red or bottle-green. The rear waist had a tightening strap edged in red, or bottle-green, along with two vertical pockets displaying three buttons. The back of Soldier's greatcoats were plain.

After 1909, the greatcoat was changed to stone-grey or field brown. Coat collars lost their piping, and collar patches were used – these were silver-grey for all Cavalry. As well, after 1909, the Officer's collar was silver-grey, and there was no additional piping.

▲ Left: Officer's greatcoat back waist decorations. Right: A 1907 illustration of the Cavalry Ferik: General de Division[14]. Cavalry Generals wore a version of the Dragoons' single breasted tunic with full-red collars and pointed red cuffs. Three woven heavy gold tape ending in a French pointed trefoil knot over the cuff identified a Ferik. Gold shoulder cords were worn as an additional form of distinction, when epaulettes were not being worn.

---

14   Sevket, 1907.

A large Bashlik, almost identical to the Russian version, was traditionally worn in winter conditions as part of the greatcoat dress. It appears to have originated as early as the Crimean War. Made from thick blanket wool. A 1909 illustration shows a Soldier wearing a large red Bashlik over their shoulders[15]. It is likely the reverse had coloured sides, the other side being grey-brown. The red side was likely for use in winter storms to help identify a Soldiers' location.

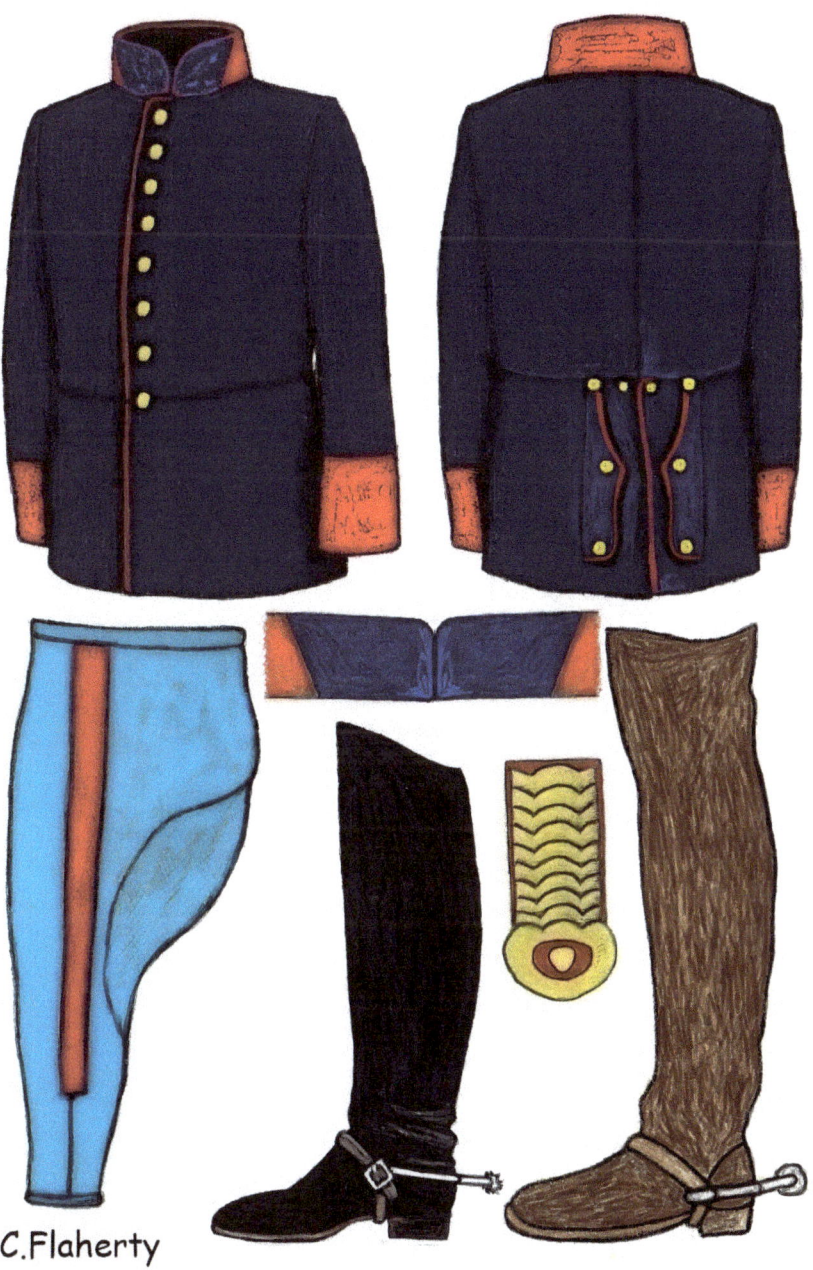

▲ The Imperial Army uniform tunic (back and front), with collar patch details, and Nefer: Private Soldier's and Junior Officer's gilt metal shoulder scales with red Ottoman-Turkish five numeral, for the 5th Cavalry Regiment. Light blue riding breeches, black knee-high, and brown long riding boots.

---

15   Ruhl, 1914.

▲ Pre-1908 photograph of a 1st Lancers Regiment Bimbashi: Major in full-dress uniform[16], identified by the three-gold stripes on his cuff-patch, as well by the epaulettes which have a loose fringe.

---

16   Private Collection, 1908.

▲ Full-dress Cavalry Ferik: General de Division, in the 1st Lancers Regiment uniform showing epaulette detail.

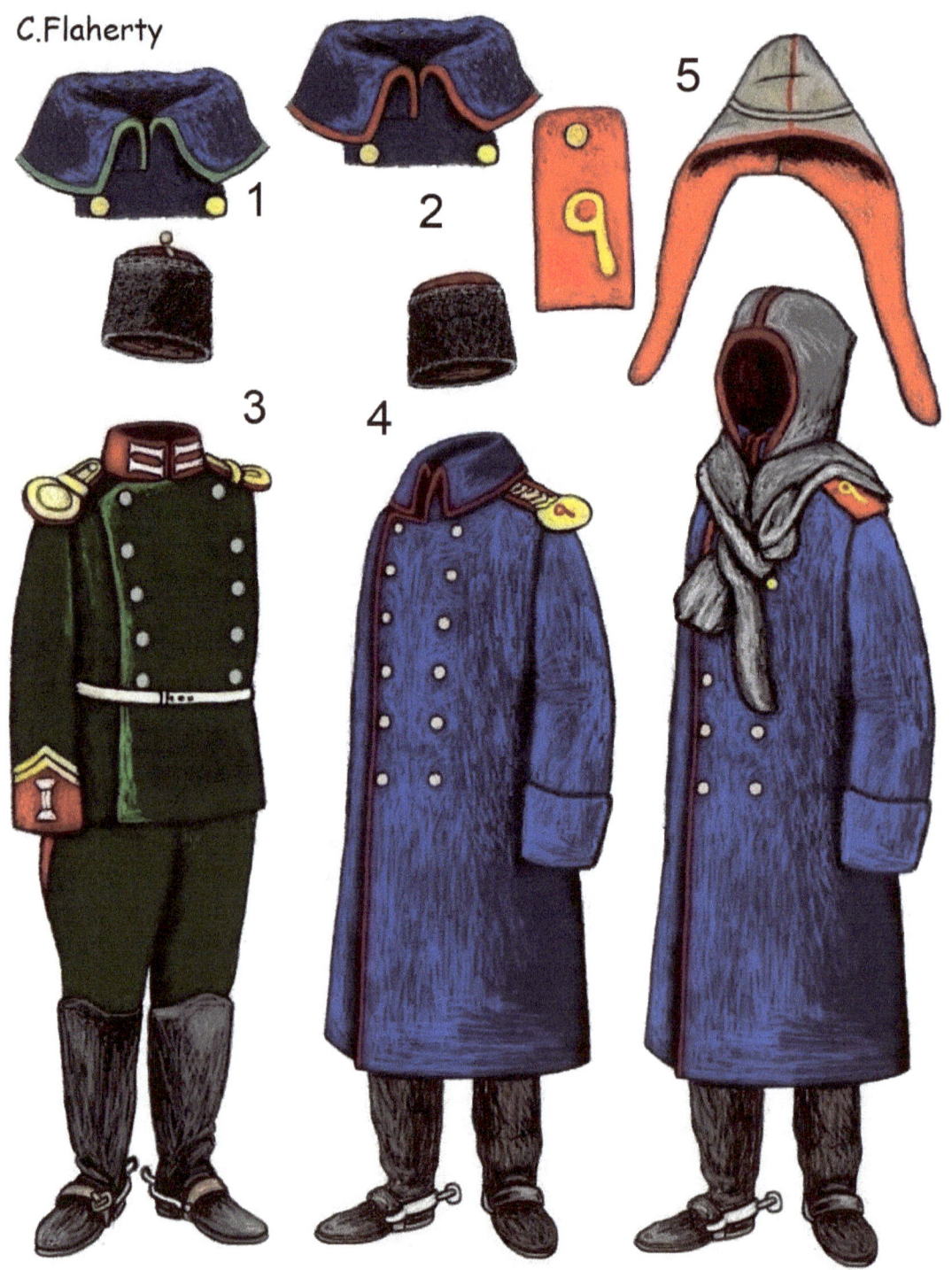

FIGURE 1: Greatcoat collar for 4th Cavalry Regiment.
FIGURE 2: Greatcoat collar for Cavalry Regiments.
FIGURE 3: Ertugrul Officer with pointed cuffs tunic version and 1861 era insignia.
FIGURE 4: Cavalry Soldier wearing a greatcoat with shoulder scales fitted.
FIGURE 5: Cavalry Soldier in greatcoat with red shoulder boards, wearing the large Bashlik, and unwrapped Bashlik details, and possible appearance of Cavalry Soldier's greatcoat shoulder board with Regimental numeral.

CHAPTER 2: OFFICER'S RANK INSIGNIA

During the time of Sultan Abdul Hamid II, there were 31 Marshals and 468 Generals in the Imperial Army, which has become known as the Army of General's Period. Following the 1860s, where the post-Crimean War Army adopted a system of cuff chevrons to indicate rank, the Sultan Abdul Hamid II era saw introduction of two more rank systems depending on the uniform being worn[17][18][19]. If the Officer was wearing a uniform with pointed cuffs, then the 1860s system was used. If the Officer's uniform had round cuffs (Cavalry Dragoon Officers), and Ertugrul Regiment for a certain period, then rank was shown as a system of gilt and silver vertical lines displayed on a large rectangular blue (green for the Ertugrul) cuff patch, edged in red (bottle-green for the 4th Cavalry Regiment) piping, with a row of five small buttons down the rear edge. Rank was also shown on the epaulettes, held with gold or silver tape bridles, and shoulder boards for the underdress uniforms option, which used a system of metal stars to indicate rank. A 1908 reference shows all Cavalry Officers were distinguished with double Russian or German gold (silver for the 1st Lancers and Ertugrul Regiments) collar bars, and a cuff button tab in gold or silver[20]. The 1st Lancers and Ertugrul Regiments Senior Officers are shown distinguished by red collars with a double silver line edge, and line of silver laurel leaves around the collar. The 4th Cavalry Senior Officers had bottle-green collars with gold lines and laurel leaves around the collar. Generals wore collar bars, or were distinguished with a red collar edged with gold double lines, and branching oak leaves around the collar.

GENERALS RANK INSIGNIA

Till 1908, Cavalry Generals wore a Dragoons' single breasted tunic with full-red collars and pointed red cuffs[21]. Whereas an 1895 illustration of Riza-Bey - Commandant de Cavalerie, with the rank of a Ferik: General de Division, shows wearing a 1st Lancers Regiment tunic with a red paraderabatte extending down the waist to the base of the skirt (not unlike the Austro-Hungarian Trabanten Leibgarde uniforms at the same time, around 1896[22]), that may have had gold piping around the edge, pointed red cuffs, collar, and epaulette bridles with gala uniform gold embroidery consisting of branching oak leaves surrounded by a double gold edge[23]. Kalpak with a red dome with gold tape stripes, blue trousers, and black riding shoes with spurs completed the dress.

▶ A 1900s example of a cuff patch rank insignia for an Army Ferik: General de Division. The cuff patch had a scalloped edge for a General. All other Officers who wore cuff patch rank insignia such as in the Dragoons had strait edges. Four embroidered gilt vertical lines indicated the rank of Miralai: Colonel). Generals wore an additional two, three, or four overlaying diagonal ones to show the wearer's rank[24][25]. The cuff button tab in this example is highly embroidered in leaves – much like the gala uniform cuff and collar gold leaves embroidery. Regular Officers' cuff button tab was formed with metallic tape.

---

17   Sevket, 1907.
18   Askeri Muze, 1986.
19   Turker, 2022.
20   Askeri Muze, 1986.
21   Sevket, 1907.
22   Unknown, 1896.
23   Le Petit Journal, 1895.
24   Ruhl, 1900.
25   Druck, 1905.

▼ **Cuff insignia for a Cavalry Liwa: General de Brigade and Ferik: General de Division. General's gala uniform collar details, Turkish and German or Russian styled collar bars. Cavalry Officers' gold (or silver for the 1st Lancers and Ertugrul Regiments) shoulder cords.**

The 1861 rank system was used, and three woven heavy gold tape ending in a French pointed trefoil knot over the cuff identified a Cavalry Ferik: General de Division, while two tape knots identified a Cavalry Liwa: General de Brigade. On the gala uniform cuffs the rank chevrons were reduced to thin gold cord. Cuffs are depicted as plain, however it is more likely these displayed a cuff button tab. Generals' epaulettes had a stiff-wire fringe. Generals' underdress shoulder boards were edged in two gilt lines and displayed like the epaulettes one star for a Cavalry Liwa: General de Brigade, and two stars for a Cavalry Ferik: General de Division.

Cavalry Generals, like all Cavalry Officers wore gold (or silver for the 1st Lancers and Ertugrul Regiments) shoulder cords on a red shoulder board as an additional form of distinction when epaulettes were not worn[26]. No rank stars or other form of distinction was displayed on these cords.

OFFICERS RANK INSIGNIA (TILL 1908)

Cavalry Major to Colonel ranks' underdress shoulder boards were edged in a gilt line. Cavalry shoulder boards were red, except for the 4th Cavalry Officers that had bottle-green fields. Epaulettes were gold, except for the 1st Lancers, and Ertugrul Regiments which were silver. An all gold (silver for the 1st Lancers, and Ertugrul Regiments) portapee was used by the Major to Colonel ranks.

MAJOR TO COLONEL		CUFFS:	LOOSE FRINGED EPAULETTES:
Miralai	Colonel	Four Gilt Lines	Three Stars
Kaimakam	Lieutenant-Colonel	Two Gilt, Two Silver Lines	Two Stars
Bimbashi	Major	Three Gilt Lines	One Star

Cavalry Lieutenant to Adjutant-Major ranks' underdress shoulder boards were plain. Up till 1876, the Cavalry had the following commissioned Officers: Second Lieutenant, First-Lieutenant, and Vice-Captain[27]. After 1876, the three Officers' ranks corresponded into Third Lieutenant (as the lowest grade Officer in the Cavalry), following the Second and First-Lieutenants. Epaulettes were fringeless. Third-Lieutenant's epaulettes had a red field with a small silver star (rank stars were commonly gilt metal), the crescent and tape edging around the red strap was silver. It is assumed Third-Lieutenant's epaulettes in the 4th Cavalry had bottle-green field and strap, and gold metal work and

---

26   Askeri Muze, 1986.
27   Roubicek, 1978.

tape. The portapee cord was black, and the acorn gold. The acorn was silver for the Officers in the 1st Lancers, and Ertugrul Regiments.

LIEUTENANT TO ADJUTANT-MAJOR		CUFFS:	FRINGELESS EPAULETTES:
Kolagasi	Adjutant-Major	Two Gilt Lines	Three Stars
Yuzbashi	Captain	Gilt and Silver Lines	Two Stars
Mulazim-i-Evvel	Full-Lieutenant	One Gilt Line	One Star
Mulazim-i-Sani	Second-Lieutenant	One Silver Line	Small Silver Star
Mulazim	Cavalry Third Lieutenant	Plain Cuff Patch*	No Star

* A plain cuff patch for an Officer is stated to be for a Kolagasi Muavinleri: Assistant Adjutant-Major[28]. This shows a blue round cuff, with red top piping, and a plain red cuff patch for the Infantry low ranked Officer.

▲ Shoulder boards, used till 1908 for a Cavalry Ferik: General de Division and Liwa: General de Brigade. Dragoon Officers' epaulettes, shoulder boards, cuff ranks, and portapee for Miralai: Colonel; Kaimakam: Lieutenant-Colonel; Bimbashi: Major; Kolagasi: Adjutant-Major; Yuzbashi: Captain in the 4th Cavalry Regiment; Mulazim-i-Evvel: Full-Lieutenant; Mulazim-i-Sani: Second Lieutenant; Mulazim: Cavalry Third Lieutenant (for the 1st Lancers Regiment).

28   Askeri Muze, 1986.

▼ 1861 cuff ranks used by Officer's in the Ertugrul and 1st Lancers Regiments. Miralai: Colonel; Kaimakam: Lieutenant-Colonel; Bimbashi: Major; Kolagasi: Adjutant-Major; Yuzbashi: Captain; Mulazim-i-Evvel: Full-Lieutenant; Mulazim-i-Sani: Second Lieutenant; Mulazim.

JUNIOR OFFICERS

Junior Officer's rank insignia began to simplify and transition from cuff-ranks to right sleeve rank chevrons, which clipped-on with hooks[29][30]. One to four large red chevrons for all Cavalry, or bottle-green for the 4th Cavalry Regiment, were worn. Earlier versions of the chevrons had brass reinforcing strips, which had the side hooks soldered-on. A top hook was provided to attach the point of the chevron just under the shoulder board edge, on the tunic's sleeve seam:

Bascavus	Sergeant-Major	Four sleeve chevrons
Bascavus Muavini	Assistant Sergeant-Major	Three sleeve chevrons
Cavus	Sergeant	Two sleeve chevrons
Onbasi	Corporal	One sleeve chevron

Below the rank of Onbasi: Corporal there was the Nefer: Private Soldier[31].

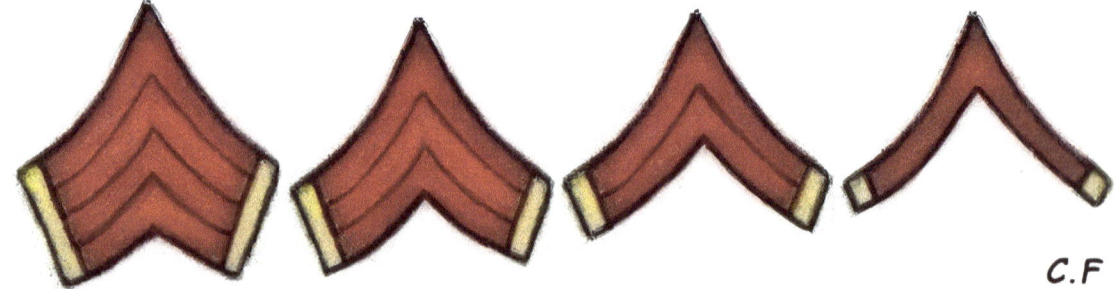

AIDES-DE-CAMP TO THE SULTAN

The 1895 illustration of Riza-Bey - Commandant de Cavalerie, shows him as an, "Aide-de-Camp de S.M.I. le Sultan."[32] Aides-de-Camp to the Sultan uniform insignia had two forms. It was a special gold aiguillette[33], and it was a gold star, crescent, or a star and crescent badge worn above the cuff. Aides-de-Camp to the Sultan had a number of functions. The Sultan's aiguillette was used in its conventional sense as a working symbol of a Staff-Officer's authority. The Sultan's aiguillette was also granted as an honour to various Officers and Soldiers. For instance, an annually published index

29	Askeri Muze, 1986.
30	Ruhl, 1900.
31	War Office, 2008.
32	Le Petit Journal, 1895.
33	Askeri Muze, 1986.

of the Government listed not only all the conventional Battalion and Regimental Adjutants, but as well all the Lieutenants, Captains who were also entitled: Aides-de-Camp Honraires[34]. It appears the title raised the status of these Officers, indicating the importance associated with the role. Ottoman military ranks carried a corresponding aristocratic title. In the case of a Lieutenant's rank, this was normally Effendi. However, a Lieutenant entitled Aides-de-Camp Honraires, was able to end his name with the aristocratic title of Bey, which was normally intended for the Major's rank and above. All Officers and Soldiers in the Sultan's Palace Guard were awarded the aiguillette, and cuff badge as part of their uniform, as were the Soldiers and Officers of the Kanun: Law Soldiers; whose judicial function differed from that of Army Police, as they specifically enforced Religious Laws in the Imperial Army.

The award of the Honorary Aide-de-Camp continued after 1908. In 1919, Mustafa Kemal Pasha writes in his memoir the importance of his position and status as the, "Hero of Anafartalar" after the Gallipoli campaign; and his title of Fahri Yaver-i Hazret-i Sehriyari: Honorary Aide-de-Camp to His Majesty Sultan"[35]. By that time, the Aides-de-Camp to the Sultan uniform insignia was likely to have included an oval sunburst with a five-point star in the centre worn on the collar, as well as over the cuffs.

▲ **Aides-de-Camp to the Sultan aiguillette and cuff insignia variations on gala uniform cuffs. Gala uniform epaulette bridle. Tunic worn by Riza-Bey - Commandant de Cavalerie (1895).**

---

34   Annuaire Oriental Du Commerce, 1891.
35   Mango, 1999.

◄ Post-1909 Army epaulettes used metallic tape edging with red highlights (previously epaulettes were plain gold). The epaulette strap is 5.6 centimetres wide, and the whole epaulette is 16.7 centimetres long. The crescent at its widest is 10.4 centimetres. The gold wire fringe is 9.7 centimetres long. No button is displayed at the end of the strap. A wire hook is mounted on the underside passing through a small pocket at the top of the shoulder. Bridles secure the base of the epaulette.

▼ Part of 'The Ertugrul Cavalry Regiment crossing the Galata Bridge', painted by Fausto Zonaro in 1901.

CHAPTER 3: IMPERIAL GUARD CAVALRY

Like the Imperial Guard Infantry, the Cavalry were also double assigned from the 1st Ordu: Army and consisted of the following four Cavalry Regiments:

IMPERIAL GUARD CAVALRY REGIMENTS	
Ertugrul Cavalry Regiment	Staff, Band, and Lead-Squadron
1st Regiment of Lancers	Taken from 1st Ordu: Army
2nd Guard Cavalry Regiment	Taken from 2nd Cavalry Regiment (1st Ordu: Army)
5th Guard Cavalry Regiment	Taken from 5th Cavalry Regiment (1st Ordu: Army)

A 1892 publication only mentions stationed in the Constantinople Garrison, forming part of the 1st Ordu: Army's Military District, "[the] … Guard Regiments … known respectively as the Ertoghrul and Rehmunut Regiments"[36]. It also states the 1st to 6th Line Cavalry Regiments were part of the 1st Ordu: Army's Military District. The 2nd and 5th Guard Cavalry Regiments appear in 1893 photographs[37]. An 1893 photograph shows the entire Ertugrul Regiment as possibly a full unit of four Squadrons[38].

Oddly, Ertugrul Regiment Officers and Soldiers wore different uniforms, with some of the Soldiers wearing 1st Lancers uniforms without the paraderabatte used. This suggests the Ertugrul had a separate Regimental Staff with less Squadrons than the 1st Lancers, and used some of their Squadrons to make up its numbers (double assigned). After 1909, the Ertugrul Regiment became the Squadron sized, "Leibgarde-Kavallerie-Regiment – Ertogrul"[39]: Sultan Mehmed V Mounted Bodyguard Troop.

▶ Special large Ertugrul Cavalry tunic button (30 millimetres diameter).

1ST REGIMENT OF LANCERS AND REHMUNUT REGIMENT

The Rehmunut Regiment, appears to be the 1st Regiment of Lancers. However, there was also a Remont Regiment in the Cifteler Harasi: Stud Farm which bred around three-hundred horses a year for the Imperial Army[40]. The 1st Lancers' uniform retained its features from the 1840s which consisted of a blue veste: shell-jacket with white metal buttons, red collar, pointed cuffs, and lapels,

---

36	Callwell, 1892.
37	Freres, 1893.
38	Freres, 1893.
39	Ruhl, 1914.
40	Askeri Muze, 1986.

▲ 1st Lancers Regiment Nefer: Private Soldiers' tunic, cuff button tab, parade silver aiguillette, Soldier's epaulette, 1897 Lancers' belt, and paraderabatte details. There appears to have been two different versions of the collar bar, one (possibly earlier) version with a closed hole on a red collar, and another showing a red highlight on a red tab, covering the front of a dark blue collar.

as a special distinction on the front of the jacket – all edged with white tape. Tape was lost around the 1870s, and a white Russian or German bar was added to the collar, and button tab to the cuffs[41]. The 1st Lancers Regiment uniform had been updated, along with the rest of the Imperial Army to a dark blue tunic that resembled the German-Bavarian Chevaulegers' tunic over the same period, with red piping, white metal buttons, with a pair arranged near the shoulder, and six more on either side. The tunic was either made with a red paraderabatte, or this was a separate buttoned-on item. Nefer: Private Soldiers, and Junior Officers' epaulettes with red cloth fields and white metal trim were worn. A German-styled cloth red with blue centre line Lancers' belt was added around 1897.

ERTUGRUL CAVALRY REGIMENT OF THE IMPERIAL GUARD

Ertugrul Regimental Staff Officers wore green German-Bavarian Chevaulegers styled tunics without the red paraderabatte, and special large white metal buttons displaying a coat of arms. Collars and cuffs were red. There were two (possibly three) versions of the Ertugrul Officers' uniform. The uniform version with round cuffs and cuff patches also had red piping down the right side of the

41   Sevket, 1907.

tunic front[42]. A 1901 painting shows round cuffs, but no tunic piping[43]. The pointed cuff version had no piping on the front[44]. The same feature is seen in an 1893 photograph[45].

Like the Officers uniform changes, the uniform worn by Junior Officers, and Nefer: Private Soldiers parading with the Ertugrul Regiment also saw several changes. A 1901 painting shows at least one Squadron in green uniforms like the Officer's version, with no paraderabatte, showing only plain fronts with two rows of large silver buttons and round red cuffs[46]. An 1896 illustration of a, "Lieb-Cav.-Reg. Ertogrul Unteroffizer"[47], shows a dark blue tunic with full red collar, red paraderabatte, with large silver buttons, with gilt metal shoulder scales, and blue round cuffs with red piping around the top, and red vertical cuff patch, with two buttons (top and bottom), identical to the Infantry tunic. An 1893 photograph shows the same cuff, but without the paraderabatte visible[48]. Breeches are dark blue with broad red side stripes. The Kalpak dome is shown as red with silver tape stripes, like the 1st Lancers Regiment. A 1908 reference shows a full red collar with a white Russian or German collar bar, with a red light for both the 1st Lancers and Ertugrul Regiments, along with the same pointed red cuffs with a white button tab on a blue sleeve[49]. A 1908 reference shows the Ertugrul Regiment wore silver metal shoulder scales[50].

▶ Ertugrul Cavalry Officer's round cuff insignia details for a Bimbashi: Major, and large Ertugrul Cavalry button.

SULTAN MEHMED V MOUNTED BODYGUARD

Called the, "Sultan Escort Squadron"[51], in service after 1909, the Sultan Mehmed V Mounted Bodyguard Troop, or Squadron were identified as the Leibgarde-Kavallerie-Regiment - Ertogrul showing their link to the former Ertugrul Cavalry (Lancers) Regiment. British references identify: "lances are carried by the Bodyguard Squadron"[52], and are shown parading in a 1914 photograph with their lances[53]. A 1916 reference mistakenly states the uniform was red with white cords, and white Kalpak[54]; however, this was the uniform of the Palace Company of Bodyguard Infantry. A light blue dolman-jacket, with black knots, and double sleeves, with a red inner sleeve is known[55]. A

42	Askeri Muze, 1986.
43	Zonaro, 1901.
44	Sevket, 1907.
45	Freres, 1893.
46	Zonaro, 1901.
47	Unknown, 1896.
48	Freres, 1893.
49	Askeri Muze, 1986.
50	Askeri Muze, 1986.
51	Roubicek, 1978.
52	British General Staff, 1995.
53	Army and Navy, 1914.
54	British General Staff, 1995.
55	Askeri Muze.

post-1909 photograph of two Officers shows dark (possibly dark blue) breeches[56]. Soldiers wore lower grade Officer's gold fringeless epaulettes. The black Kalpak was fitted with gilt chin scales and attachment bosses, had a black cloth dome with gold tape stripes, and being a high quality item these may have had red highlights. The Kalpak badge consisted of a star and crescent over two pairs of lances tied together. A 1917 photograph[57], and film shows a tall white egret feather plume used[58]. The Sultan Mehmed V Mounted Bodyguard Troop Soldiers also wore the new 1909 Army Officer's suit (with six buttons), in olive green cloth, or a white (summer wear version), with full red collars, and shoulder boards, with dark blue breeches and riding boots[59]. The Kalpak badge appears changed to a large crescent and star. The pre-1908 era red right sleeve rank chevrons were also worn. Large silver Ertugrul buttons were likely still used.

▲ A variation Ertugrul troop Kalpak badge mounted on a small buckle. Possibly used as a belt.

▲ The 1st Regiment of Lancers in 1895[60].

56   Unknown, 1909.
57   German Official Photographer, 1917.
58   Critical Past.
59   Ruhl, 1914.
60   Knotel, 1895.

▲ The 1909 Sultan Mehmed V Leibgarde-Kavallerie-Regiment – Ertogrul: Mounted Bodyguard Troop's ceremonial, field and summer dress uniforms.

FIGURE 6: Ertugrul Cavalry Officer with round cuff rank insignia.

FIGURE 7: 1st Lancer Nefer: Private Soldier (till 1908).

FIGURE 8: Dragoon Officer, showing Kalpak dome details (till 1908).
FIGURE 9: 1st Lancer Mulazim: Third-Lieutenant (till 1908). Showing collar bar details.
FIGURE 10: Ertugrul Nefer: Private Soldier with white metal shoulder scales. Showing the Infantry cuff used on one tunic version.

FIGURE 11: Nefer: Private Soldier in blue uniform (this uniform could also be green) parading with the Ertugrul Cavalry, using an Ertugrul Regiment's horse schabracke.

FIGURE 12: Ertugrul Troop Officer (after 1909), showing the horse schabracke details.

CHAPTER 4: DRAGOONS AND CUIRASSIERS

Worn for duty in the Palace[61], the 1880s version of the Dragoon uniform used a plain double-sleeve buttoned jacket with a short skirt. It had a standing red collar, and plain shoulder boards.

The 1861 predecessor was a long skirted tunic, with hidden buttons, and fall-down collar, and its outer blue sleeve had coloured cuffs – red, white, dark red, and green to distinguish each Regiment in the Ordu: Army Cavalry Division. Use of the Palace duty uniform may relate to the 2nd and 5th Cavalry Dragoon Regiments assigned to the Imperial Guard. After 1880, Line Dragoons adopted the new blue suit.

▶ Dragoon Bimbashi: Major's Palace duty uniform double sleeve details[62]. Officers outer sleeve vents were edged in gold cord. A Soldier's shoulder board.

4TH CAVALRY REGIMENT

The 4th Dragoon Cavalry Regiment was uniformed as a Mounted Rifles Cavalry unit following from the 1850s Chasseurs-a-Cheval (Horse Rifles) and wore bottle-green facings.

LINE LANCERS

Following 1879, the first Regiment in each of the Cavalry Divisions carried lances[63]. There was no special insignia, except for the Regimental numbers used. It is known, from 1879, a Cavalry Division was active in the first five Ordu: Army military regions[64]. The remaining Line Lancer Regiments, were likely to be the: 7th (2nd Ordu: Army); 13th (3rd Ordu: Army); 19th (4th Ordu: Army); and, 25th (5th Ordu: Army). In the First World War, it was reported that the 6th and the 8th Regiments of Lancers (3rd Cavalry Division), were present at the 1917 Battle of Beersheba[65]. The same Regiments is also stated, "did not exist"[66].

CUIRASSIERS

A photograph (taken between 1880 and 1893) from the, "Interior of the Weapons Museum" - Armory Museum of Ayairene (Church of St. Irene), shows a number of full sets of French cuirass, and

---

61	Askeri Muze, 1986.
62	Askeri Muze, 1986.
63	Askeri Muze, 1986.
64	Roubicek, 1978.
65	Falls, 1930.
66	British General Staff, 1995.

helmets with star and crescent finals[67]. The same items were photographed again around 1920[68]. The Imperial Army is said to have planned to form Cuirassier Regiments. It is said, the project were abandoned due to the high costs of maintaining the Regiment, and difficulty finding suitably large horses, as it was known at the time Imperial Army horses were under-sized, and not suited to shock tactics[69]. To be a Cuirassier, the Soldiers themselves would have needed to have been at least six feet tall.

FIGURE 13: Line Dragoon Nefer: Private Soldier wearing their Palace duty uniform.

---

67   Unknown, 1880.
68   Pyhrr, 1989.
69   British General Staff, 1995.

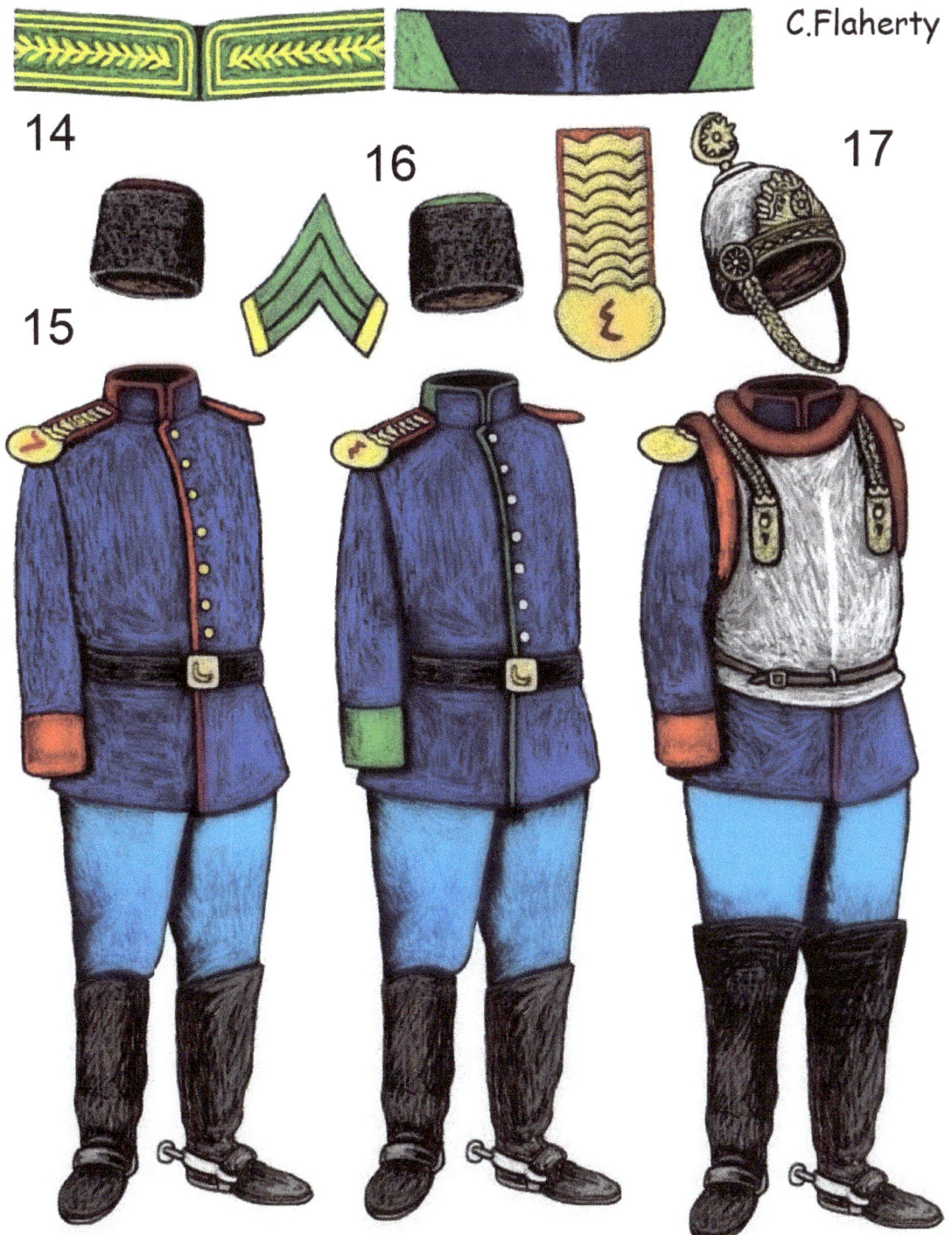

FIGURE 14: 4th Cavalry Regiment Senior Officer's gala uniform collar details (till 1908). 4th Cavalry Regiment Soldier's collar details.
FIGURE 15: Line Dragoon Nefer: Private Soldier (till 1908).
FIGURE 16: 4th Cavalry Regiment Nefer: Private Soldier, with Junior Officer's shoulder chevrons, and Soldier's gilt shoulder scales details.
FIGURE 17: Possible appearance of the Experimental Cuirassier (1879).

CHAPTER 5: LINE DRAGOON CAVALRY AFTER 1909

From 1909 the Line Dragoon Cavalry, along with the rest of the Imperial Army adopted a new field brown suit that had a short standing collar (Officers had a wide folded-down coloured collar), with breast and hip pockets. The Officers' tunic had six buttons down the front, while Soldiers had five. Brown cloth riding breeches with narrow red tape side stripes, and black riding boots completed the dress. Soldiers adopted a small yellow brown Kalpak with silver grey domes. Officers continued to wear black Kalpak. Silver grey facings, with gilt buttons, were now worn by all the Cavalry. Regimental numbers were displayed on Junior Officers and Nefer: Private Soldiers' collars (on the right-side collar tab), and the Officers' shoulder cords[70]. At the start of the First World War there were over twenty Dragoon Cavalry Regiments. These were not numbered consecutively:

Regiments:	2nd, 3rd, 4th, 5th, 6th, and 7th.
Regiments:	11th, 12th, 13th, 14th, and 15th.
Regiments:	19th, 20th, 21st, 22nd, 23rd, 24th, 25th, 26th, and 27th.
Regiments:	29th, 31st, and 33rd.

▲ A sellection of 1909 era Officer's shoulder cords for Generals, Major to Colonel ranks, and Lieutenant to Captain ranks.

---

70   British General Staff, 1995.

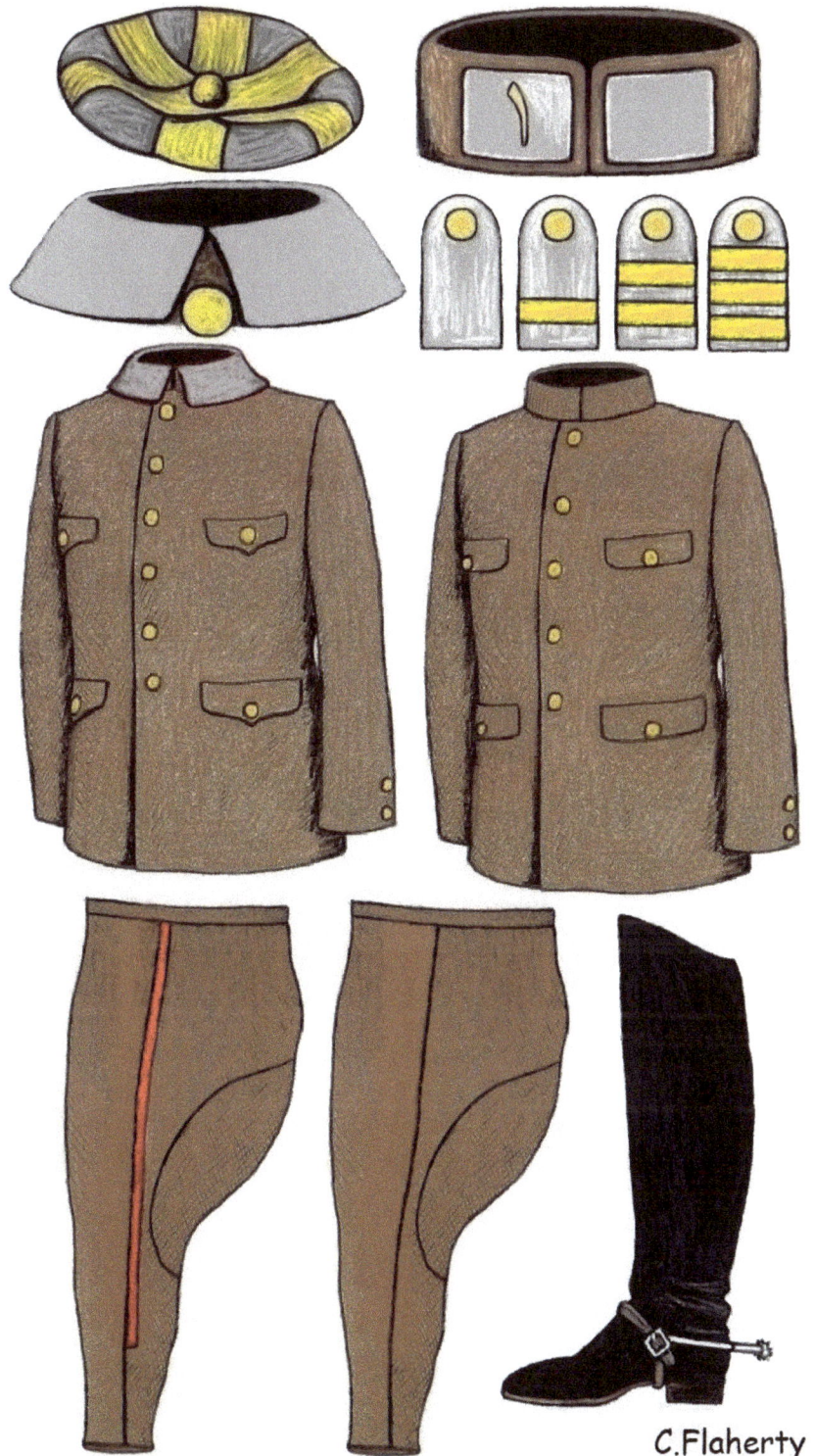

▲ The post-1909 Officer's and Soldier's tunics. Showing details for the collars, with the 1st Regiment's numeral. Officer's Kalpak dome (Soldiers wore plain versions without the gilt tape star design), and Onbasi: Corporal's rank shoulder board. Cavus: Sergeant had one gilt stripe across the board; Bascavus Muavini: Assistant Sergeant-Major (two stripes); and Bascavus: Sergeant-Major (three).

▲ Post-1909 Turkish Dragoon Nefer: Private Soldier in summer light-weight version of uniform.

CHAPTER 6: HEJAZ DIVISION CAVALRY

The 22nd Cavalry Regiment had two Squadrons which may have been camel, or mule mounted for operating in the desert, along with some of the Infantry mounted on mules. After 1879, the only distinctive uniform feature of the 16th Hejaz Division Troops was wearing the Keffiyeh, held in place by a rope circlet, called an Agal. At that time, items like the Keffiyeh were generally worn throughout the Empire, and the bigger the tassels, the more value it had, and the higher the wearer's status. A wide selection of white, black Keffiyeh are seen worn in early photographs, that also show many traditional Yemeni designs and colours used as well. Till 1908, the 16th Hejaz Division Troops' Keffiyeh was a red-and-white checkered pattern[71], which also had decorative cotton or wool tassels on the sides. The Agal displayed a separate pinned-on Hamidiye cast brass coat of arms badge, which had been adopted in 1882. The hot climate conditions in Hejaz would have seen widespread use of 1860s era white summer, and fatigue uniforms. An illustration titled: Ottoman Army Soldiers during the 1877 Russo-Turkish War[72], shows Turkish Soldiers wearing a white smock, not unlike the French colonial service white fatigue uniform of the time. The Infantry Soldier's white fatigue uniform consisted of a low open collared garment that was closed by a short vent with two large buttons. The shirt cuffs were also closed around the wrist with a button. The front of the smock was heavily pleated. The smock hem came down to the wearer's calves. Loose white pants, and waist band completed the dress.

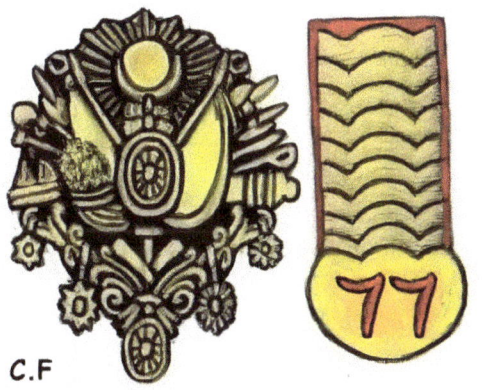

C.F

◀ Hejaz Division 22nd Cavalry Regiment Hamidiye coat of arms badge, and gilt shoulder scales details.

▼ Two examples of the 1882 Hamidiye cast brass coat of arms badge (7x5.8 centimetres), has a copper button with a Tugra for Sultan Abdul Hamid II. Underneath a very small RUMI year 27 (٢٧) of rule (1901/1902). Indicating when it was cast. Pinned and stitched to a square of red wool cloth possibly cut from a Fez. The next example is 1901 dated fully cast brass badge (7x5.8 centimetres).

---

71 Askeri Muze, 1986.
72 Ollier, 1890.

▲ Hejaz Division 22nd Cavalry Regiment (till-1908) Nefer: Private Soldier.

▲ Hejaz Division camel mounted Nefer: Private Soldier wearing summer fatigue uniform (till-1908), with a locally made civilian Keffiyeh.

▲ A Hejaz mule Mounted Infantry Nefer: Private Soldier wearing protective driver's goggles. In the First World War, there were several Mounted Infantry Battalions in Syria and Mesopotamia[73]. On 13 March, 1916 an Estersuvar: Mule Cavalry Regiment was formed under the 53rd Infantry Division. Using a Turkish Cavalry saddle originally covered by its schabracke, and traditional tribal Arab harness. Artillery Drivers' saddles were also likely used.

73   British General Staff, 1995.

▲ A photograph taken between 1908 and 1914[74], shows a Mounted Infantry Soldier using a makeshift saddle and harness, including a cord-rope loop used as stirrups.

74   Private Collection, 1914.

CHAPTER 7: HAMIDIYE CORPS

Established by, and named after Sultan Abdul Hamid II in 1890, the Hamidiye Corps (meaning: belonging to Hamid), had the full official name Hamidiye Hafif Suvari Alaylari: Hamidiye Light Cavalry Regiments, that incorporated Foot Companies, operating as a type of mounted, or dismounted Dragoons. The Hamidiye Corps were under the command of the Asakir-i Hamidiye Komutani, who was a Ferik: General de Division, and attached to the 4th Ordu: Army. The Asakir-i Hamidiye Komutani was assisted by two Miralai: Colonels. Imperial Army Officers commanded Regiments and Squadrons. Tribal Chiefs of Regiments had the rank of Bimbashi: Major.

CIRCASSIEN VOLUNTEER CAVALRY

The 1860s Circassien Volunteer Cavalry uniform served as the basis for the Hamidiye Corps. A 1907 illustration of the Circassien Volunteer Cavalry Squadron uniform shows wearing a classical version of the Cossack dress, complete with a large Busby (displaying a large upwards pointing crescent badge), this also had a red cloth flap with yellow lines[75]. Soldiers wore a blue long flowing wrap around frock coat, with red chest pockets for spare cartridges. A red short, collared shirt was worn under this. The coat and chest pockets were trimmed in yellow tape. Red Russian pants and soft brown-yellow boots completed the uniform.

HAMIDIYE CORPS OFFICERS

Hamidiye Corps Officers are depicted wearing a Kalpak with a red dome, and gold tape stripes, displaying on the front a gilt metal Hamidiye (Sultan Abdul Hamid II) cast brass coat of arms badge[76]. The uniform consisted of a long blue buttonless coat, with blue collar and pointed cuffs. The breast had blue chest pockets for decorative cartridge bottles. Wide gold tape edged the collar, cuffs, chest pockets, and coat edge. Light blue pants, with wide gold tape side stripes can be seen in a photograph of a Bimbashi: Major in the Kurdish Hamidiye[77], left loose over the riding boots, or could be tucked into these[78][79]. Gold shoulder cords, or red shoulder boards edged in gold cord, displayed rank stars. Lower grade Officers had plain red shoulder boards[80]. Officer's used the 1861 rank system on their cuffs.

A 1908 illustration shows the Tribal Chief of the Karapapak Tribe Regiment[81], listed below in the table of Tribes and Barracks, as number 6, with the rank of Bimbashi: Major, displaying three gold cuff chevrons, and red shoulder boards edged with gold, with one gold star. An 1896 photograph of the Karapapak Officers, also shows the Dragoons' tunic worn with a dark (possibly dark blue) collar edged with wide gold tape, which could also be double Russian or German gold collar bars[82]. An 1895 photograph of Officers at a Review of Kurdish Cavalry by the Governor of Van, Bahri Pasha[83], shows wearing a Dragoons' tunic with pointed cuffs displaying the 1861 rank system, Kalpak with Hamidiye coat of arms badge, and rank shoulder boards. An 1890 photograph of a Miralai: Colonel

---

75	Sevket, 1907.
76	Askeri Muze, 1986.
77	Unknown, 1901.
78	Askeri Muze, 1986.
79	Lynch, 1901.
80	Lynch, 1901.
81	Askeri Muze, 1986.
82	Servet-i-Funun, 1896.
83	Greene, 1895.

shows a crescent badge displayed above their cuff insignia signifying their status as an Aide-de-Camp to the Sultan[84].

HAMIDIYE CORPS SOLDIERS

The 1895 photograph of the Review of Kurdish Cavalry shows the Soldiers wearing their own clothing. It is also known, Tribal Cavalry each had to provide their own horse, and saddle equipment[85]. An 1891 photograph of, "Le Regiment de la Cavalerie Hamidie de Kiss a Ourfa"[86], shows Arab Cavalry wearing their own clothing, and the Hamidiye coat of arms badge displayed on the Agal. Located at Ourfa, this suggests this was the Tay (Arab) Regiment, listed below as number 46, barracked at Nusaybin some 140 miles away.

SWORDS

Hamidiye Corps commonly wore a Cossack Shashka, and Kindjal Swords[87]. The Kindjal was a gladius sword 81 centimetres long (total length); its blade was 65 centimetres; and the blade width was 5.5 centimetres. The weapon was suspended at the front, at an angle from a narrow decorative metal plate waist belt[88]. The Cossack Shashka was either suspended from the same belt, or from a shoulder sling-strap. Uniquely, the Turkish version of the Shashka had a high metal mouthpiece on the scabbard that covered most of the sword handle.

HAMIDIYE REGIMENTS (TRIBES AND BARRACKS)

The Hamidiye Regiments were organised into 57 Hamidiye Light Cavalry Regiments (Dragoons)[89][90], and were stationed in towns and villages[91]. There were some 65 Tribes providing Regiments. The units were well-armed, and consisted of Irregular Sunni Kurdish, Turkish, Turkmen and Yoruk Cavalry that operated in the Eastern provinces of the Empire. While classed as Cavalry, they were mixed Infantry and Cavalry Brigade-sized Battalions.

▶ Regiments were organized as half Infantry and Cavalry Companies:

▶ Where the Regiment had more than 600 Officers and Soldiers:

1st Infantry Company
2nd Infantry Company
3rd Mounted Company
4th Mounted Company
5th Mounted Company

---

84 Unknown, 1890.
85 British General Staff, 1995.
86 Servet-i-Funun, 1891.
87 Askeri Muze, 1986.
88 Lynch, 1901.
89 Askeri Muze, 1986.
90 Kodaman, 2011.
91 Varli, 1995.

After the overthrow of Sultan Abdal Hamid II in 1909, the Hamidiye Cavalry was disbanded as an organized force. However, a few select units were kept in Government service. Among these were all-Kurdish units renamed as Tribal Regiments, in the Imperial Army, and deployed to Yemen and Albania.

▼ **Kurdish Cavalry Officers wearing a Dragoons' tunic. Possible appearance of a Hamidiye Cavalry Nefer: Private Soldier based on two 1917 photographs of a Staff-Orderly Car Driver[92][93], for Jamal [Cemal] Pasha - leader of the Turkish Army against the British forces in Egypt, Palestine and Syria in the First World War. The photographs show a Soldier-Driver wearing a low double buttoned collared shirt with a long plain open collarless Cossack coat. A Kalpak, with the Hamidiye coat of arms badge, and boots completes the dress. In the photographs the Driver wears a narrow waist belt with a Kindjal Sword suspended from it. A Turkish version of the Shashka details.**

---

92   American Colony of Jerusalem, 1917.
93   German Official Photographer, 1917.

▼ Hamidiye Corps Regiments' Number, Tribe, Location, Cavalry, Infantry Totals:

1	Sipkan	Dutak	400	250	650
2	Sipkan	Hosuna	400	175	575
3	Sipkan	Cemal Verdi	400	225	625
4	Zilan	Toprakkale	250	360	610
5	Zilan	Karakilise	450	250	700
6	Karapapak and Kurds	Eleskirt and Karakilise	400	150	650
7	Terekeme and Kurds	Tulak-Karakilise	300	200	500
8	Kesvan	Hasankale	200	175	475
9	Sapikan and Badayan	Kızıldiz	250	325	575
10	Taskesen and Diyadin	Kasatkanlı	198	350	548
11	Mikaili	Karakilise and Diyadin	175	325	500
12	Hamdiki, Basimi, Hal Hesini	Karakilise and Diyadin	225	350	525
13	Haydaran	Bergiri (Muradiye)	200	318	518
14	Haydaran	Bergiri (Muradiye)	175	350	525
15	Sevli	Van and Timar	200	350	550
16	Kalıkan	Ercis	255	270	525
17	Mukuri	Saray	215	315	530
18	Takari	Zermaniz and Saray	300	380	680
19	Milli and Semsiki	Saray	225	425	650
20	Skeftka	Eblak	327	213	540
21	Adaman, Zilan, Hecidıran	Ercis	250	275	525
22	Haydaran	Ercis	175	350	525
23	Haydaran	Adilcevaz	200	350	550
24	Heydaran	Ercis	175	350	525
25	Marhoran	Adilcevaz	250	300	550
26	Hasenan	Hınıs (Kumdeban)	335	205	540
27	Hasenan	Malazgirt	340	200	540
28	Hasenan	Malazgirt (Diknuk, Dinbut)	304	230	534
29	Hasenan	Morankoyu	310	230	540
30	Hasenan	Bulanik	308	232	540
31	Cibran	Gumgum	308	232	540
32	Cibran	Hinis	310	235	545
33	Cibran	Varto	315	330	545

34	Zirkan	Tekman	300	250	550
35	Zirkan	Soylemez	375	500	875
36	Cibran	Kigi	285	265	550
37	Celali	Bayezit (Ortulu Kislagi)	305	370	540
38	Celali	Bayezit (Seyhlu Kislagi)	300	240	540
39	Takori	Mahmudiye (Saray)	305	301	606
40	Kafkasya Muhacirleri	Sivas	275	500	775
41	Milli	Mardin	275	265	540
42	Milli	Siverek	255	375	630
43	Milli	Siverek	303	247	550
44	Karakeci	Siverek	305	225	530
45	Kikan	Ra's al-Ayn, Mardin	350	270	620
46	Tay (Arab)	Nusaybin	445	185	630
47	Karakeci	Siverek	310	230	540
48	Miran	Cezire	335	205	540
49	Miran	Cezire	308	232	540
50	Ertosi	Elbak	375	300	625
51	Kays	Urfa	450	200	650
52	Kays	Harran	400	150	550
53	Berazi	Urfa	250	300	550
54	Berazi	Urfa	300	300	600
55	Berazi	Urfa	275	300	575
56	Gevdan	Hakkari	200	300	500
57	Sadili	Hasankale	300	250	550
58	Adaman	Ercis	200	350	550
59	Pinyan	Hakkari	150	400	550
60	Sidan	Hakkari	350	300	650
61	Kasıkan	Soylemez	250	300	550
62	Kiki	Harran	250	350	600
63	Milli	Viransehir	550	250	800
64	Milli	Viransehir	600	225	825
65	Belideyi	Ercis, Patnos, Malazgirt	250	200	450

▲ Hamidiye Cavalry Tribal Chief, with the rank of Bimbashi: Major (1890 till 1908).

CHAPTER 8: MOUNTED GENDARME

Beginning in the late 1840s, as the Zaptiye: Mounted Police, the new troops had a much more expanded role with the Army providing, "a valuable body of 30,000 men"[94][95]. They were described as:

> "[A] … Gendarmerie force which served in small detachments all over the Empire in a para-military Police type role. They could, however, be Brigaded together as a Cavalry force and apparently some such units served in the Crimea in this function."[96]

Between 1861, and 1876, eight Gendarmery Regiments were created. The Regiments were known by their geographical titles[97]:

HISTORICAL TITLE	MODERN DAY LOCATIONS	
Brousse Gendarmery Regiment	Bursa	North-Western Anatolia (Turkey)
Smyrne Gendarmery Regiment	Izmir	Province Capital Western Extremity of Anatolia
Angora Gendarmery Regiment	Ankara	Central Anatolia
Kastamonia Gendarmery Regiment		Capital District of Kastamonu Province (Turkey)
Konia Gendarmery Regiment	Iconium	City in South-Central Turkey
Trebizond Gendarmery Regiment		Black Sea Coast City North-East Turkey
Hejaz Gendarmery Regiment		Region in the West of Saudi Arabia
Yemen Gendarmery Regiment		South Arabia

OFFICER'S UNIFORMS AND RANK INSIGNIA

From 1879, Provincial Cavalry Gendarmery Officers, till 1903 wore a dark blue dolman jacket with dark blue pointed cuffs with gold cords, cuff ranks chevrons with French-styled sleeve trefoil knots using gold cord-work, and blue collars edged in double gold cords[98]. Dark blue riding breeches with wide gold double tape side stripes, black riding boots, and Fez completed the dress. Officers in addition to their cuff rank insignia were further distinguished wearing gold dress shoulder cords. Using the 1861 era rank insignia system, the gold and silver cord cuff chevrons combinations, were worn under a gold triple cuff knot as an extra form of distinction:

Gendarme Mulazim-i-Sani: Lieutenant	One silver cord cuff chevron
Gendarme Mulazim-i-Evvel: Full-Lieutenant	One gold cord cuff chevron
Gendarme Yuzbashi: Captain	Two gold cord chevrons
Gendarme Bimbashi: Major	Two (one gold, one silver) cuff chevrons

---

94   Dodd, 1856.
95   Cox, 1997.
96   Cox, 1997.
97   Roubicek, 1978.
98   Askeri Muze, 1986.

Gendarme Kolagasi: Adjutant-Major	Three gold cord cuff chevrons
Gendarme Kaimakam: Lieutenant-Colonel	Four (gold, silver, gold, silver) cord cuff chevrons
Gendarme Miralai: Colonel	Four gold cord cuff chevrons

From 1903, the Gendarme Officer wore a cornflower blue dolman jacket with scarlet collars and pointed cuffs[99][100]. The cords were black. Officers wore cornflower blue pants, or riding breeches, with wide tape black side stripes. A black Kalpak, with a scarlet dome, and black riding boots completed the dress. The Officers in addition to their cuff rank insignia were further distinguished wearing gold dress shoulder cords or Army Officer's epaulettes. The 1903 new uniform stayed in use till the First World War. The Officer's rank insignia used the 1861 era system, but embellished with a black sleeve triple knot.

ORDINARY GENDARMERY UNIFORMS

Up till the late 1870s, both Turkish and Egyptian Gendarmery were dressed in light blue Zouave Uniforms with yellow facings, and red infill pockets. From 1879, Provincial Cavalry Gendarmery, till 1903 wore the same uniform as the Officers, except the dark blue pointed cuffs were top edged with yellow cord and knot, like the rest of the dolman jacket's cords. Junior Officers ranks were displayed on the collar: Gendarme Onbasi: Corporal (one star); Gendarme Adjutant (two stars); Gendarme Cavus: Sergeant (three stars); and, Gendarme Bascavus: Sergeant-Major (four stars)[101]. Cavalry Gendarmery in Constantinople wore a dark blue tunic with gilt buttons – not unlike the Infantry Soldier's tunic. The collar was dark blue with red front tabs, and the front of the tunic had red piping down the opening vent. Round dark blue cuffs edged with red piping around the top, also had red tri-pointed cuff patches with three gilt buttons (the Infantry version used a rectangular cuff patch with two buttons). Dark blue riding breeches with narrow red tape side stripes, black riding boots, and Fez completed the dress. Ordinary Gendarme in the Constantinople Cavalry Regiment wore a red aiguillette[102]. In regards, to the Officers in the Cavalry Gendarmery in Constantinople, as the Soldiers wore buttoned cuff patches it appears they may have worn the five buttoned version that displayed rank using stripes.

A 1916 publication describes the uniform of the pre-First World War ordinary Gendarme, and that of the Officers by that time, that came into use after 1903 (while the Officers still wore the dolman):

> "Uniform.-Single-breasted jacket of cornflower blue, with scarlet collar patches. Trousers of the same stuff and colour as the jacket. The winter suit is of serge, the summer suit of a cotton twill. Black Kalpak with scarlet top and silver stripes".[103]

The 1903 uniform appears to have been the 1876 version of the Cavalry Gendarmery in Constantinople's uniform except in cornflower blue, including use of round cornflower blue cuffs edged with red piping around the top, also having red tri-pointed cuff patches with three gilt buttons.

99	Graphic, 1904.
100	Graves, 1933.
101	Askeri Muze, 1986.
102	Askeri Muze, 1986.
103	British General Staff, 1995.

FIGURE 18: Constantinople Cavalry Gendarme Regiment's aiguillette details (till 1903).
FIGURE 19: Turkish or Egyptian Mounted Gendarmery (till 1879).
FIGURE 20: Star and crescent belt buckle commonly used by Gendarmery.
FIGURE 21: Provincial Gendarme Cavalry Yuzbashi: Captain's cuff rank (till 1903); and, Constantinople Cavalry Gendarme Regiment Boluk Eminleri: Company Commander's sleeve chevrons details (till 1903).
FIGURE 22: Provincial Gendarme Cavalry Adjutant (till 1903); with collar details for a Gendarme Private Soldier, Onbasi: Corporal; Adjutant; Cavus: Sergeant; and, Bascavus: Sergeant-Major.

FIGURE 23: Constantinople Cavalry Gendarme (till 1903).

FIGURE 24: Provincial Gendarme Cavalry Yuzbashi: Captain (till 1903).

FIGURE 25: Gendarme Yuzbashi: Captain (after 1903), showing the horse schabracke details.

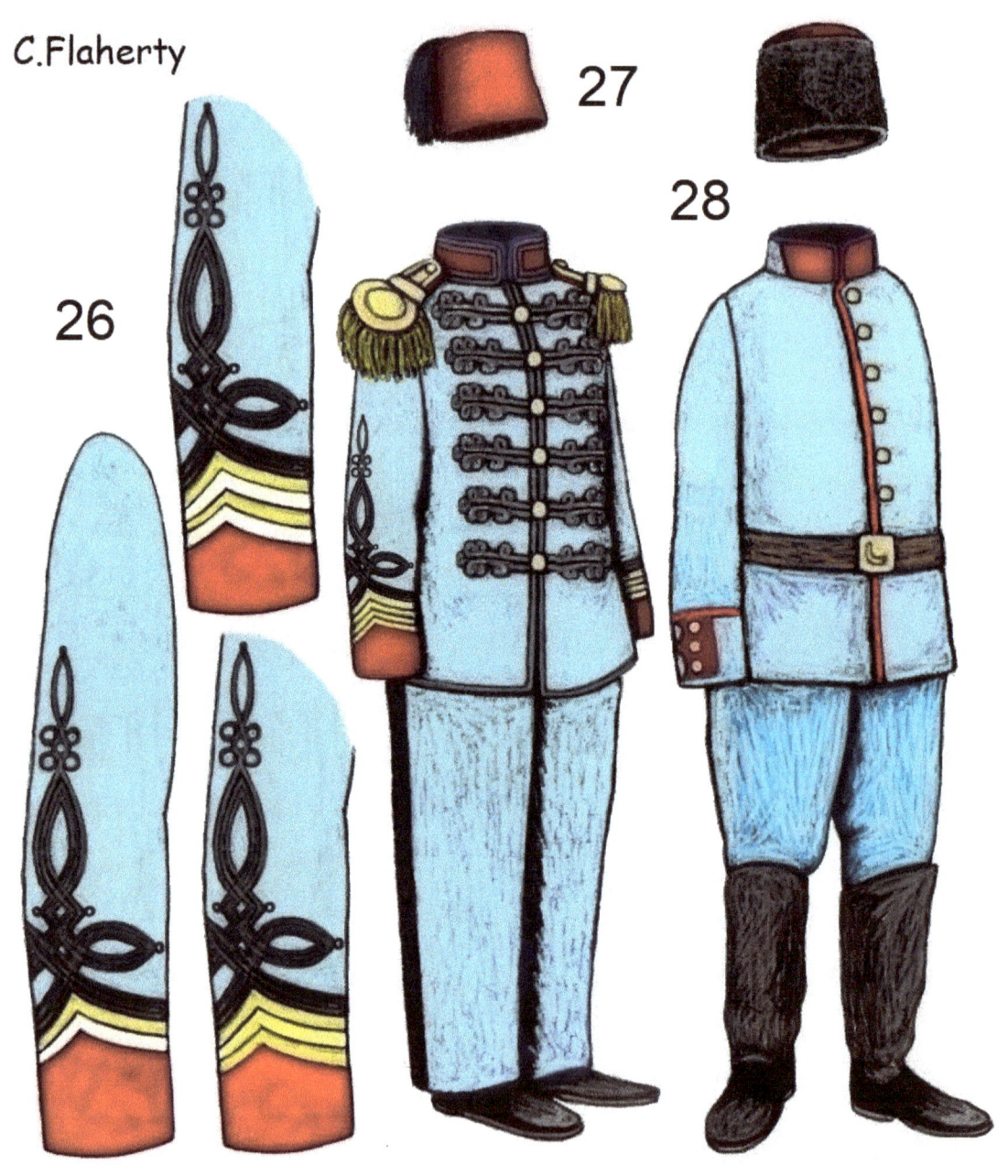

FIGURE 26: Gendarme sleeve and cuff rank details for: Kaimakam: Lieutenant-Colonel; Gendarme Bimbashi: Major; and, Gendarme Kolagasi: Adjutant-Major (after 1903).
FIGURE 27: Gendarme Miralai: Colonel (after 1903).
FIGURE 28: Ordinary Gendarme (after 1903).

CHAPTER 9: CAVALRY ARTILLERY

By 1879, the Imperial Army's Artillery was largely divided into Field, and Garrison Branches. In most European Armies the old distinction between Mounted, Field and Positional Batteries was being abolished as the rifled field gun revolution saw introduction of limber-caisson wagons with seating for the Gunners, and Gunners riding on horse teams. During the Greco-Turkish war of 1897, Ferik Viktor Karl Ludwig von Grumbkow (Pasha von Grumbkow) promoted the development of a Flying Artillery Column with added horses for rapid movement. The 1st Mobile Artillery Bodyguard Brigade, consisting of two full Companies of Mounted Gunners crewing a six-gun Field Artillery Battery, was Brigaded with the Imperial Guard as a Cavalry Artillery. The only uniform distinction appears to have been wearing the Cavalry cross-belt slung cartridge box from the 1861 era[104]. It displayed a large flaming grenade, attached to chain and arrow pick, and crossed cannon badge with stacked balls, and crescent. Longer soft German or Russian styled Cavalry boots covering the knees were worn as a further distinction.

The 1879 Artillery were uniformed in an almost direct copy of the French Army's Artillery, wearing a dark blue dolman jacket with red pointed cuffs, and red collars. All cords decorating the jacket were black[105][106]. Light blue riding breeches with wide red tape side stripes, black riding boots, and Kalpak with a red dome completed the dress.

▶ The 1897 Von Grumbkow's Cavalry Artillery uniform was different from earlier Field Artillery General's uniforms which had round cuffs and cuff patches to show the Officer's rank. The Von Grumbkow uniform used Cavalry Generals' 1861 cuff rank insignia with pointed red cuffs. This version displays a gala uniform cuff with extra gold embroidery. The Turkish made Artillery button was a direct copy of the French Field Artillery tunic button used at the same time. A Mobile Artillery Bodyguard Officer's cross-belt slung cartridge box details.

---

104   Askeri Muze, 1986.
105   Druck, 1905.
106   Askeri Muze, 1986.

▼ Cavalry Artillery Ferik Viktor Karl Ludwig von Grumbkow (Pasha von Grumbkow), wearing an Officer's 1st Mobile Artillery Bodyguard Brigade uniform in 1897[107].

107   Bartlett, 1897.

▲ An earlier tunic for a Field Artillery Ferik: General de Division. It has round cuffs, with cuff patches to show the Officer's rank. The buttons are back marked: ONNIK & CIE BRODEURS DE LA COUR. This is the Constantinople Imperial Court Jewellers Lazian Onnik. This tunic belonged to Ristow Pasha, who was a German Officer, promoted to Ferik in command of the Field Artillery, from 1885 till 1890, when he died from an accident holidaying in Germany. While the cuffs and collar embroidery are Turkish patterns, the tunic body, and its cross cannon and grenade buttons is identical to a French Field Artillery uniform used at the same time.

▲ Cavalry Artillery Soldier (till 1908).

CHAPTER 10: SULTAN'S STANDARD AND CAVALRY SANJAKDAR

Called, the Sultan's Standard, a universal pattern banner, was awarded to each Army Regiment, between 1843, and 1844, by Sultan Abdulmecid, in order to bring his newly organized Army closer to European styled Regiments, each with its own standard[108]. All Regiments - Infantry, Cavalry or Artillery, received identical flags, in two patterns – the 1844, and later the 1882 version. The 1844 Sultan's Standard is thought to have been a high quality red banner displaying a silver crescent badge on a red field[109]. Though star and crescent versions are also commonly depicted. The new 1882 standards given to all Imperial Army Regiments by Sultan Abdul Hamid II incorporated a state coat of arms – the Hamidiye in gold on a red field, with a gold fringe edge. Banners were attached to a black wood pole topped with a gilt crescent finial. Over the same period, the banner's leather bandoleer was covered with red cloth, and edged with gold tape.

SANJAKDAR: STANDARD BEARER OFFICER

The 1843 Turkish Army Organization Laws saw the rank of Sanjakdar: Standard Bearer Officer abolished[110]. However, each Battalion or Regiment still had an Officer dedicated to carrying the unit flag. Personally responsible for the Sultan's Standard, its care, maintenance, protection, and usually commanded an attending squad of two to five Soldiers to protect the flag. The Sanjakdar was a comparative rank to a British Army Ensign, and were still identifiable in the First World War[111]. The Officer is listed in seniority as below a Regimental Clerk Officer, and above the rank of Sergeant-Major. A Flag Cavus: Sergeant at the Company level were also known.

A 4th Cavalry Regiment Sanjakdar Officer is depicted in an 1897 illustration wearing an Officer's tunic without epaulettes, but possibly wearing a Mulazim-i-Sani: Second-Lieutenant's shoulder boards[112]. The collar is shown as plain without bars, and the pointed cuff has an 1861 silver cuff rank chevron. The rank was further distinguished by wearing a gold embroidered red carry strap which is shown under a black leather cartridge box cross-belt. An 1893 photograph of a Ertugrul Lieutenant Sanjakdar shows wearing a plain single breasted tunic with large buttons and Mulazim-i-Sani: Second-Lieutenant's epaulettes[113]. Pointed cuffs have a 1861 silver cuff rank chevron, and there are collar bars.

▶ A 4th Cavalry Regiment Sanjakdar Officer (1897).

108	Hacisalihoglu, 2007.
109	Deroy, 1855.
110	Roubicek, 1978.
111	British General Staff, 1995.
112	Demoulin, 1897.
113	Freres, 1893.

An 1893 photograph of a 2nd Guard Cavalry Regiment Lieutenant Sanjakdar shows wearing a plain single breasted tunic[114]. Another 1893 photograph of a 1st Lancer Lieutenant Sanjakdar shows wearing a single breasted tunic with buttoned black chest-loops that end in trefoil knots[115]. While another 1893 photograph of a 5th Guard Cavalry Regiment Lieutenant Sanjakdar shows the tunic with the same chest loops[116].

SULTAN ABDUL HAMID II SPECIAL AWARD BANNER

The four Imperial Guard Cavalry Regiments used the following standards:

Ertugrul Cavalry Regiment	Sultan Abdul Hamid II Standard
1st Regiment of Lancers	Sultan Abdul Hamid II Standard
2nd Guard Cavalry Regiment	Sultan Abdul Hamid II Standard
5th Guard Cavalry Regiment	Sultan Abdul Hamid II Special Award Banner
First Mobile Artillery Bodyguard Brigade	Sultan Abdul Hamid II Special Award Banner

An 1893 photograph of Sultan Abdul Hamid II Special Award Banners for the First Mobile Artillery Bodyguard Brigade shows gold script text in a box divided into five bars[117]. An 1893 photograph of the 5th Guard Cavalry Regiment's banner had a line of script along the top over two boxes with three lines of script[118]. A banner illustration show a green field, gold script and fringe edge[119], while an 1895 illustration shows a red field with large silver script and fringe edge[120]. Illustrations and photographs show staffs with a large ball finial topped with a large circular crescent. The 1893 photographs only show a small portion of the script text used on the banners. Quran text is known from the Special Award Banner of the 79th Infantry Regiment who defended Gaza, Palestine, in 1917[121]. Another green silk rectangular panel contains three lines of cream (faded gold) script from the Quran surrounded by a square border[122].

1909 SULTAN MEHMED V RESHAD STANDARD

The 1909 Sultan Mehmed V Reshad standard given to all Army Regiments was a crimson silk field with a coiled and linked gold bullion fringe. Embroidered in gold bullion thread with the Tugra of Sultan Mehmet V within a circle surrounded with representations of four regimental flags and various military symbols, including pikes, double-headed axes and trumpets. Suspended, from a scroll of leaves are five green embroidered cords hanging five medals. The gold embroidered reverse side displayed the Shahada: "There is no God but God, and Mohammed, the Messenger of God". Attached to the staff are: "two gold bullion and crimson silk cords and tassels."[123] The staff finial was highly crafted and represented a brass crescent with a nickel metal star.

▶ The 1843 till 1882 Sultan Abdulmecid Standard used in Turkish and Egyptian Armies.

114   Freres, 1893.
115   Freres, 1893.
116   Freres, 1893.
117   Freres, 1893.
118   Freres, 1893.
119   Knotel, 1897.
120   Knotel, 1895.
121   Askeri Muze, 1917.
122   Sakip Sabanci Museum.
123   Australian War Memorial.

▲ 1882 Sultan Abdul Hamid II standard for an Army Infantry, Cavalry or Artillery Regiment. A 2nd Guard Cavalry Regiment Cavalry Lieutenant Sanjakdar with a 1843 banner. Cloth and leather bandoleer. Mulazim-i-Sani: Second-Lieutenant's shoulder board.

▲ 1893 Ertugrul Lieutenant Sanjakdar, and 5th Cavalry Lieutenant Sanjakdar with Sultan Abdul Hamid II Special Award Banner, using part of the 79th Infantry Regiment's banner Quran text (1917). Also showing chest knot details.

▲ 1909 Cavalry Lieutenant Sanjakdar and Sultan Mehmed V Reshad standard.

HEADQUARTERS FLAGS

The Imperial Army in 1909, adopted the 1885 German black, white and red Stabsflaggen: flags to identify Army (square flag), Corps (swallow tailed), and Division (pointed) Headquarters. Modifying these for their own use changing the colours to red and white, these same flags are still in current use in the Turkish Armed Forces.

The Division Stabsflaggen was red over white. However, a version from the First World War said to belong to the 3rd Cavalry Division is a very large and long red lance pennant with a white triangle near the hoist[124]. It is more likely this was for a Cavalry Brigade Headquarters.

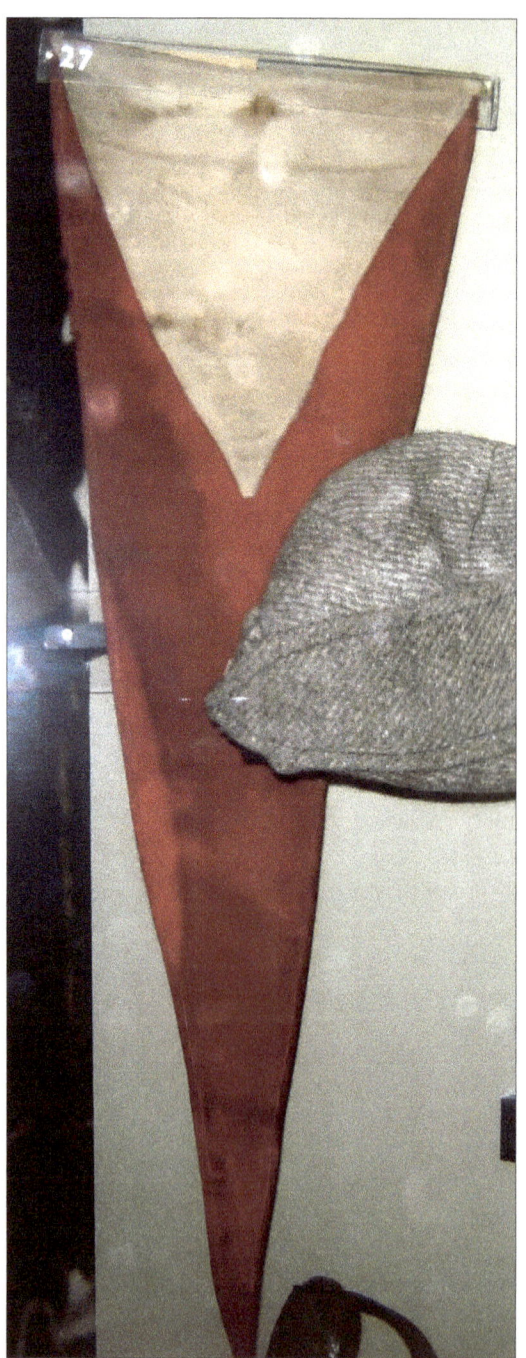

▶ A large Turkish Army lance pennant from the First World War, said to be for the 3rd Cavalry Division. However, it may be for the 3rd Cavalry Brigade Headquarters instead. Photograph credit to Chris Dale.

▼ 1909 Turkish Army Stabsflaggen for a Corps, Division, and a possible Brigade Headquarters version.

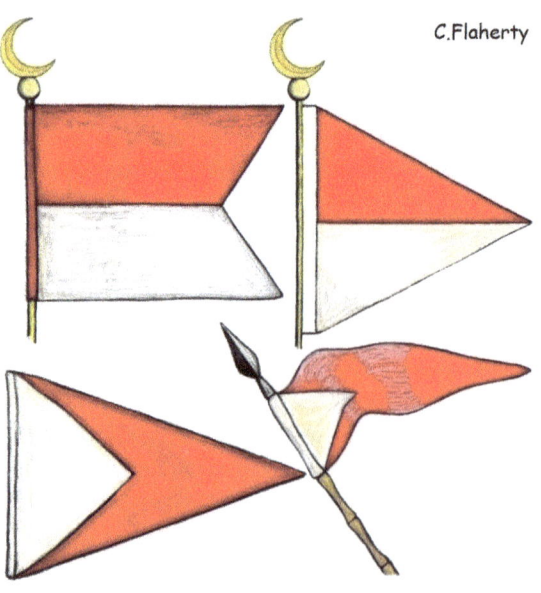

---

124   Imperial War Museum.

CHAPTER 11: EGYPTIAN CAVALRY

The 1841 edict of inheritance formalized the autonomous status of Egypt, as a privileged Province within the Empire, secured hereditary succession, and specified ways in which Turkish sovereignty should be symbolised such as the Egyptian Army and Navy wearing Turkish uniforms and parading with the Turkish flag[125]. An 1840 account lists fifteen Nizam Cavalry Regiments[126]. However, the total number of Regiments was never realised, and only two small Regiments existed in 1863[127]. An increase to eight was planned, but never fielded more than four. In 1883, the Egyptian Army had fifteen Cavalry Regiments with 500 Soldiers each[128]. Each Regiment had five Squadrons. Rather than being Nizam, the bulk of the Egyptian Army Cavalry were mounted Bashi-Bazouk.

In the 1877 Russo-Turkish War, the Egyptian Army appeared in a low rounded collared, loose-cut version of the Crimean War tunic, with pointed cuffs[129]. The Egyptian Army tunic was dark blue with white piping, and closed by six buttons. Loose dark blue pants, with piped seams, were tucked into the legwear. The Cavalry were distinguished with yellow collars and cuffs. In the summer, white uniforms were worn. Early-on, the horse schabracke was of French Napoleonic design, with long pointed green, then later blue cloths with a broad yellow, then later red border with a black sheepskin cover over the saddle frame. From the 1870s most illustrations show Mounted Troops using all leather saddles, with underside padding not unlike the British Army's version[130]. Egyptian Cavalry commonly strapped a large blanket roll to the front of the saddle. A small square blanket schabracke with a broad border with a leather saddle is shown in an 1882 illustration[131]. A pair of pistol holsters were often slung over the front of the saddle. A small sheepskin could have also been used to cover the pistol holsters.

EGYPTIAN CUIRASSIERS

Egyptian Cuirassiers wearing a steel helmet with a chainmail shirt had been a feature of the Mameluke Cavalry in the Napoleonic era. Known as the Zirkhagi: Iron Men,

> "[they were] ... once two Regiments strong, and contributors to Ibrahim's victory at Nezib (1839), they were now part of the Khedival Guard. Armed with sabres and pistols, these men wore chainmail armour and metal helmets with nose-guards."[132]

In 1883, General Hick's Cavalry force included - "100 Cuirassiers, sheathed in coats of mail resembling those worn in the middle ages."[133] The chainmail shirts appear to have replaced French made steel cuirass used during the Crimean War. It is known, in the 1880s the Khedive Tewfik (Khedive of Egypt, between 1879 till 1892), ordered from a Birmingham firm 600 hauberks made of split rings for the Egyptian Army under Hicks. The Birmingham chainmail shirts are said to have proved worse than useless. The iron rings (which resemble modern key rings), were simply interlinked, breaking and shattering when struck with bullets causing even more injury from the shrapnel. An 1882 illustration titled: "Cuirassier of the Guard" shows plain white European Cavalry gaun-

---

125 Peri, 2005.
126 Charton, 1840.
127 Dunn, 2013.
128 Lutsky, 1969.
129 **Drury, 2012.**
130 Unknown, 1883.
131 Montbard, 1882.
132 Dunn, 2013.
133 Royle, 1886.

tlets[134]. Wilkinson Sword Company Sales Catalogues from the 1860s were known to offer swordproof gauntlets for Cavalry use. An 1883 illustration of a Zirkhagi shows the right rein-hand gauntlet completely covered in chainmail; whereas, the left (sword) hand gauntlet is only partially covered in mail, leaving a leather hand portion[135], which would have been protected by the basket-hilt of the wearer's sword. French Army Heavy Cavalry swords, dating from the Napoleonic period were sold in large quantities to the Egyptian and Turkish Armies (and were still in use in the First World War). An 1883 illustration shows a Persian styled helmet from the front[136], and an 1882 illustration shows it from the sideview[137]. The 1882 and 1883 illustrations show a deep domed helmet with a separately-applied brow plate; adjustable nose-guard; and small, spiked ball-finial. Likely to be a Wilkinson sword-proof helmet, specifically made for the Egyptian Army. Helmets were supplied by companies in Birmingham. It is stated: "now in the Tower collection ... [which would now be the Royal Armouries] ... the helmet shown with which is one of many made in Birmingham for the Khedive of Egypt's Regiment of Iron Men."[138] Information from a 2012 auction catalogue indicates that they also had a deeply-domed helmet, from the Sudan:

> 'surmounted by a spike ball-finial, with separately-applied brow plate and adjustable nasal guard. Including a camail: a piece of chainmail attached to the headpiece and protecting the neck and shoulders woven of heavy split rings.'

The description of this helmet included the note: "Helmets of this type were made in Birmingham, originally for the Bodyguard of the Khedive of Egypt, known as the, 'Iron Men'"[139]. The Sudanese, it would appear, "only used the helmets they captured from the Egyptians"[140]. It also notes that in their original form, these Sudanese helmets with their long chainmail neck curtains were, "sewn to a thickly quilted lining which extends to the shoulders, across the lower face, and then down to form a cuirass which laces up under the left arm."[141] Another helmet, with the exact same form, in a Museum collection, is identified as - "Kulah Khud, Persian style helmet, circa 1898"[142]. The description makes no connection with Egyptian Army helmets from the United Kingdom, only that the helmet was taken from a Sudanese at the end of the Battle of Omdurman. This has also been altered with the addition of a brass nose-guard, permanently fixed in place, and sewn to a heavy internal quilt lining. An 1883 illustration shows the Zirkhagi uniform as broad breaches and Cavalry boots[143]. Nothing is known what uniform was worn underneath the chainmail shirts. An 1883 illustration of Egyptian Infantry show wearing a long collarless, loose long sleeved white shirt and a short open jacket[144]. It is supposed that Zirkhagi wore much the same clothing under their hauberks.

An 1883 photograph of the Guardia del Ministra: Ministers' Escort Guards[145], shows a buckle that appears to be a variation of the French Second Empire Sapeur: Engineer's buckle displaying a Roman helmet with cuirass, which suggests a connection with the Zirkhagi – who may have worn a similar uniform, as red uniforms was often associated with Khedive Guards. Shown in the photograph a flaming grenade (which was used on the French Second Empire's Cuirassier buckle) with a spread of flags with crescent finials similar to the flag pattern seen on the Khedive coat of arms, added to the design.

134	London Illustrated News, 1882.
135	Graphic, 1883.
136	Graphic, 1883.
137	Montbard, 1882.
138	Robinson, 1967.
139	Auctions Imperial, 2012.
140	Robinson, 1967.
141	Robinson, 1967.
142	National Army Museum, 1898.
143	Graphic, 1883.
144	Graphic, 1883.
145	Unknown, 1883.

Guardia del Ministra wore a red frockcoat with gold chest bars, and pointed red cuffs with gold piping[146]. Blue pants with wide double yellow side stripes, Fez, and black shoes completed the dress.

An 1843 illustration of, "Cavalerie Egyptienne" shows Zirkhagi using dark blue horse schabracke and portemanteau: valise with a white-silver tape border[147]. An 1882 illustration shows Zirkhagi using standard Egyptian Army Cavalry saddles in the period, with a blanket role strapped over the front of the saddle[148]. An 1882 illustration titled: "Cuirassier of the Guard" shows a small horse schabracke with a rounded front, and pointed end, with a narrow double tape border[149]. Two Portemanteau with double tape ends are shown strapped to the back and front.

▶ 1883 Guardia del Ministra buckle.

▼ Zirkhagi wearing full armour, along with gauntlets (1883). The next Zirkhagi shows clothing likely worn under the chainmail hauberk. The helmets' chainmail neck curtains are depicted sewn to green cloth. Egyptian Cavalry Soldier wearing the field service khaki uniform (after 1885).

---

146   Unknown, 1883.
147   Goupil-Fesquet, 1843.
148   Montbard, 1882.
149   London Illustrated News, 1882.

GENERAL HICKS 1883 EXPEDITION ARMY CAVALRY

The Egyptian Government Army formed for that year, under General Hicks, had 900 Cavalry[150]. It later received 600 more Bashi-Bazouk: Irregular Cavalry[151]. Most accounts suggest the Egyptian Government Army Cavalry was composed of its Cuirassiers, and the rest were mounted Bashi-Bazouk. By the mid-1870s, the Bashi-Bazouk in Egypt were organised into nine main bodies of 300 to 400 Soldiers, plus a large collection of smaller units[152]. An 1883 illustration showing Bashi-Bazouk Troops in Egypt identifies these as from Albania, Bosnia, Syria, and Greece[153].

The Greeks are said to have been renegade from Thessaly, in the 1877 Russo-Turkish War[154]. The last attempt to recruit Albanian Bashi-Bazouk by the Egyptian Government in large numbers ended in 1884. The Imperial Army General Staff abolished use of Bashi-Bazouk due to their disastrous use in the 1877 Russo-Turkish War[155]. An 1883 illustration shows Bashi-Bazouk Troops in Egypt wearing mostly blue Zouave uniforms with red or yellow trim (introduced in the early 1860s), used by the Imperial Army's Ilave: Reserve Infantry Battalions and Auxiliary Troops through-out the 1876 till 1908 era[156]. The Kurd Cavalry wore a sheep wool conical hat. An Albanian Officer is depicted wearing a double sleeved Zouave jacket, with broad Russian pants, and riding boots. A waist band, Fez and collarless vest opened at the top completes the dress. Balkan Bashi-Bazouk also wore a variety of coloured and embroidered vests over silk sashes, white linen shirts and trousers[157]. It is also said that their turbans were usually multi-coloured and shoes were often red.

▶ **Albanian Bashi-Bazouk Captain in Egypt (1883); and, Kurd Cavalry (1883).**

150	Ellens, 2013.
151	Royle, 1886.
152	Dunn, 2013.
153	Graphic, 1883.
154	Drury, 2012.
155	Britannica, 2025.
156	Graphic, 1883.
157	Johnson, 1972.

AFTER 1883

The loss of the 100 or so Iron Men with the rest of General Hicks' Army in 1883, never saw the unit reformed, as the Egyptian Army was entering a new phase of development under the British. The new Egyptian Army was formally raised in 1883[158]. By 1885, the Cavalry consisted of eight Troops (small Squadrons), with a strength of 71 Officers and Soldiers each. In 1891, the eight Squadrons had been reorganized into five Squadrons (with a strength of 100 Soldiers each). In 1896, an additional four Squadrons were added. In 1897, another Squadron was raised from the reserves (giving the Cavalry ten Squadrons). The Line Cavalry uniform consisted of a dark blue Lancers jacket with white collar, white square-ended shoulder boards, pointed white cuffs and white piping around the seams, and white paraderabatte. The rear vent had two pairs of buttons on either side, with back seams piping similar to a British Lancer's uniform in this period. The Imperial Army buttons were white metal. A red cloth belt with two black centrelines was worn. The dark blue riding breeches had double broad white side stripes. A Fez and black riding boots (British Army pattern) completed the dress. Officers wore a broad gold girdle with two red centrelines around the waist, and shoulder cords displaying stars and the Khedive crown badge as part of the rank system, the cords were fitted with the Egyptian Army's aiguillette. For summer wear there was a white copy of the tunic, with a white paraderabatte.

TRANSITION TO THE FIELD SERVICE KHAKI UNIFORM

The Egyptian Army white summer wear uniform had seven front buttons, and two pairs of back vent buttons[159]. Sometime in 1885 the new khaki suit was introduced as a field service uniform relegating the blue and white uniforms to barracks duty[160]. The khaki suit was dark salmon-sand coloured, loose fitting, short-skirted jacket, with six gilt-brass buttons down the front[161]. It had a low standing collar, and plain shoulder straps attached, with plain cuffs. Buttoned breast pockets were later added. The khaki pants were worn with blue puttees and brown riding shoes with spurs buckled-on. The Fez was covered by a khaki cloth puggaree and had a tie-on neck cloth. Following the 21st Lancers Regiment (British Army), who had Indian Army tri-pointed chainmail epaulettes added to their field service khaki uniforms by 1898, a 1912 reference on the Cavalry in Egypt states: "Squadrons are known by numbers, and the numeral is worn on the shoulder chains."[162]

MOUNTED ROYAL GUARD OF THE KHEDIVE OF EGYPT

The Mounted Royal Guard of the Khedive of Egypt wore a mid-blue Lancers jacket with red collar, pointed red cuffs and red piping around the seams, and red paraderabatte, with plain gilt metal buttons[163]. Officer's collars and paraderabatte were edged in gold tape. A broad gold girdle with two red centrelines was worn around the waist. A Fez and British-styled aiguillette was worn on the right-side. Mid-blue riding breeches had double broad red side stripes, and black riding boots (British Army pattern) completed the dress. The lance pennant was blue over red.

HORSE SADDLERY-KIT

After 1885, schabracke were not used by the Cavalry. Instead, the Cavalry used the British-Egyptian

---

158	Johnson, 1972.
159	Montbard, 1882.
160	Johnson, 1972.
161	Army and Navy Gazette, 1900.
162	British General Staff, 1912.
163	National Military Museum.

Army Cavalry padded saddle pattern. A mix of British Army and Imperial Army Cavalry equipment was used. By 1900, the Lancers were using the full British Army pattern horse saddlery-kit[164]. In the 1890s, the first or Lead-Squadron received lances. The lance pattern was either the British Army 1868 pattern lance made of bamboo (used until 1885), or the 1885 ash version. The 1885 British Army lance pennants was scarlet over white. From the 1840s, Egyptian Army Nizam Cavalry Regiments armed with lances, were distinguished by different pennant colours. A blue over white French lance pennant was described in 1854[165]. Later 1890s illustrations show red over white, or red over black versions[166]. A Turkish flag version can be seen in an 1899 painting showing Egyptian Lancers[167]. While an 1890 painting of, "Major General Grenfel watching the advance of the 9th and 10th Sudanese Battalions of the Egyptian Army against the Mahdists at Toski, 1889" shows an Egyptian Lancer with a red over green pennant[168]. The Cavalry cross-belt slung cartridge box was identical to the Imperial Army type. British Cavalry black sabretache with brass star and crescent badges, or Khedive crown badge were used.

EGYPTIAN ARMY RANKS

Egyptian Army Ranks prior to 1883 used a system of cuff cheverons similar to the 1861 era versions used in the Imperial Army. After 1883, the system conformed to the British Army of the period using a combination of stars and crowns displayed on shoulder boards. A metal five-point star was used not unlike the Imperial Army Officer rank insignia (used after 1879), and a unique crown badge, known as the Khedive crown. This was a Western-styled crown with a crescent, or star and crescent at its top rather than a cross.

Gold (sometimes silver are known) shoulder cords displaying rank insignia are worn by Egyptian Army Officers. The cords were combined with a special Egyptian Army's aiguillette, consisting of three cords slung across the chest connecting the shoulder cords together. A 1902 colourised photograph of a British Officer wearing their Egyptian Army uniform shows how the aiguillette cords were woven into the forward facing edge at the shoulder end of the cord[169].

▼ Aiguillette and shoulder cords for a Saghkolaghsi: Adjutant-Major Battalion Staff.

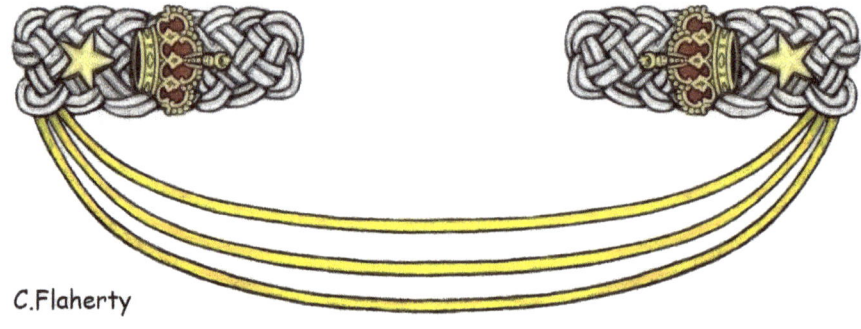

164	Army and Navy Gazette, 1900.
165	Beamont, 1856.
166	Unknown, 1898.
167	Giles, 1899.
168	Donne, 1890.
169	Lekegian, 1902.

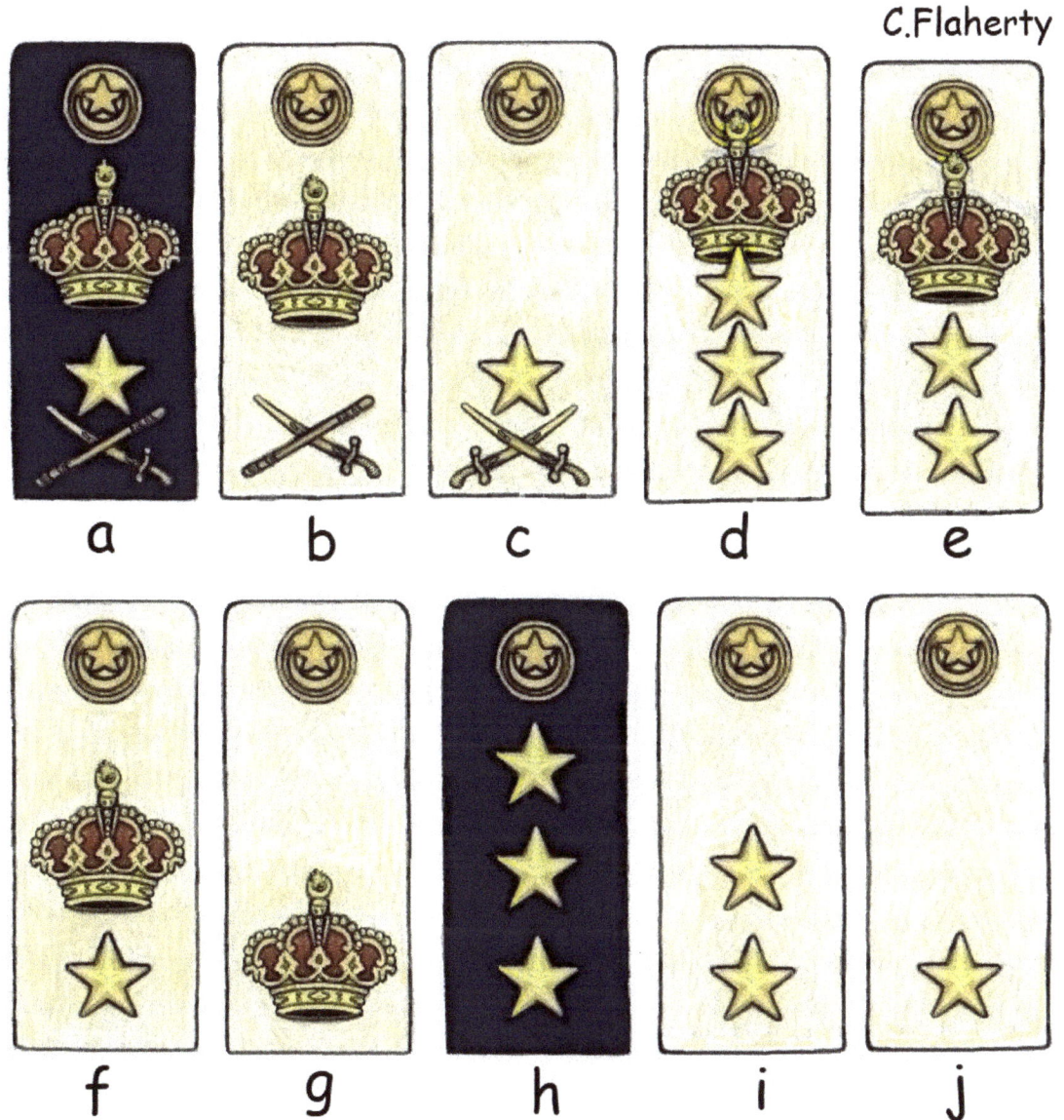

▲ Egyptian Army Ranks (after 1883): Egyptian Army Sirdar: General-in-Chief (a); Ferik: Division Lieutenant-General (b); Lewa: Brigadier General (c); Miralai: Colonel (d); Kaimakam: Lieutenant-Colonel (e); Saghkolaghsi: Adjutant-Major Battalion Staff (f); Saghkolaghsi: Adjutant-Major (g); Yuzbashi: Captain (h); Mulazim Awal: Lieutenant (i); and, Mulazim Tani: Second Lieutenant (j).

FIGURE 29: Guardia del Ministra uniform (1883). The Zirkhagi horse schabracke is shown used.

FIGURE 30: Egyptian Army Cavalry Soldier before 1883, showing saddle details.

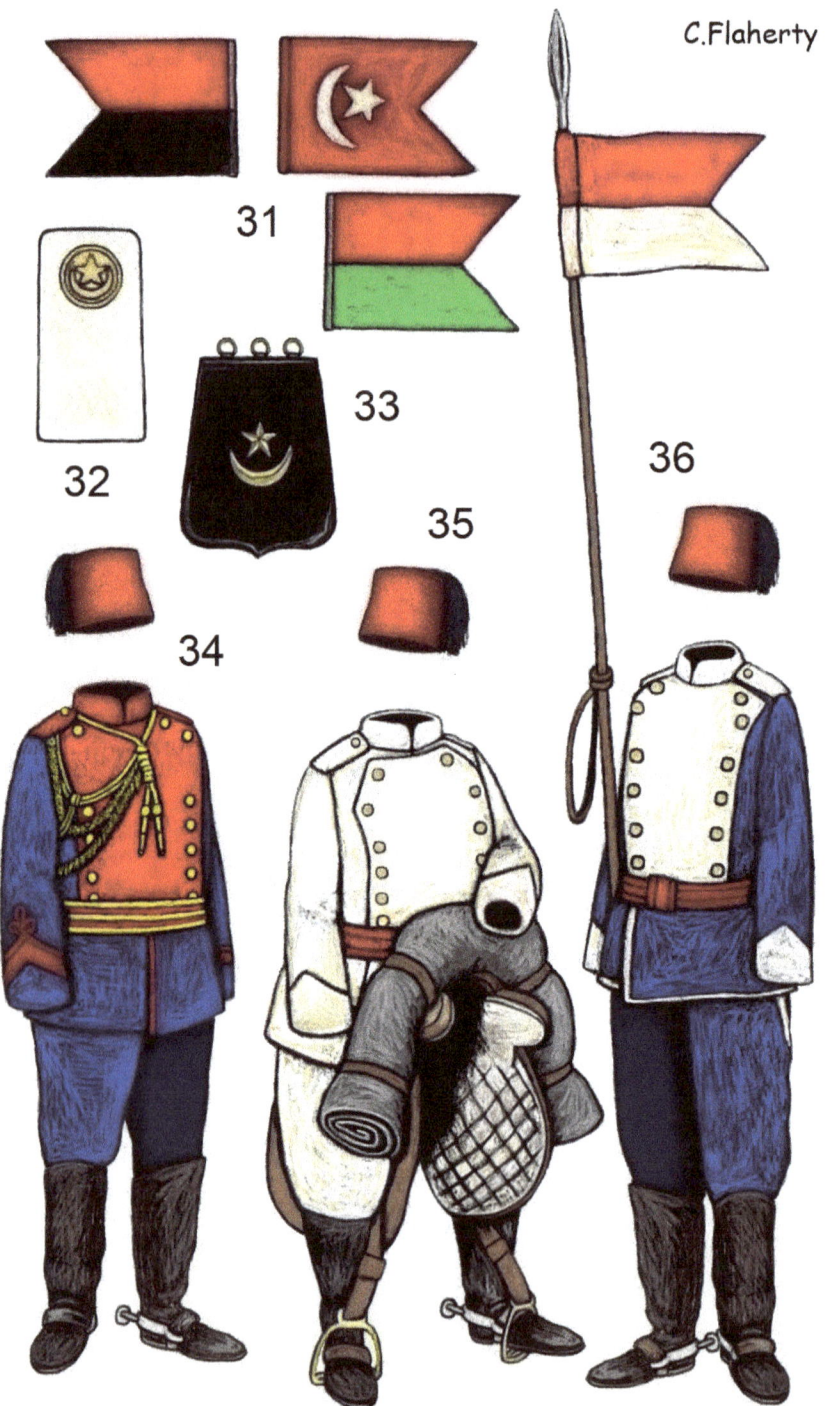

FIGURE 31: Egyptian Cavalry lance pennants.
FIGURE 32: Troopers shoulder board.
FIGURE 33: British Cavalry Sabretache used by the Egyptian Cavalry details.
FIGURE 34: Mounted Royal Guard of the Khedive of Egypt (1895).
FIGURE 35: Lancers' Summer Uniform (after 1883), and saddle details.
FIGURE 36: Lancers' full dress uniform (1895 till 1914), with an 1885 lance pattern, and likely British Army pennant, which may indicate one of the individual Squadrons.

FIGURE 37: Mounted Lancer Officer (1895), with shoulder cords, and the special Egyptian Army's aiguillette.

CHAPTER 12: EGYPTIAN ARMY CAMEL CORPS

Historically, the Egyptian Army used Camel Riders as a significant part of its transport[170]. Prior to 1884, there was one Company of Camel Troops, and one Camel Battery[171][172].

▼ Camel Corps Soldier, British Army Camel Infantry Saddle details, Egyptian Government Camel Saddle details, Camel Corps Officer (from around 1883).

---

170   Dunn, 2013.
171   Johnson, 1972.
172   Johnson, 1969.

The Egyptian Army's Camel Corps existed from early 1883, and were recruited from first-class shots within the Army, and from men already familiar with camels. It proved to be a highly successful force:

> "First raised in early days of the Egyptian Army in April, 1883, the Camel Corps was then an Irregular Corps, in which the men found their own food and clothing; it was composed of Sudanese and Egyptian Soldiers mounted entirely on Government camels."[173]

In 1885, the Egyptian Army had a total of three Companies of Camel Corps. In 1891 there were six Companies with 152 Officers and Soldiers each. The Camel Corps had originally been all Egyptians, but now included two Sudanese Companies. In 1897, the Camel Corps was increased to eight Companies (four Egyptian and four Sudanese).

▼ **Camel Corps Soldier and shoulder board details (1885).**

---

173   Boustead, 1934.

A pre-1882 illustration (that likely dates to the 1870s) shows an Egyptian Camel Troops Rider wearing a white turban, loose shirt, and white knee-length breeches[174]. Egyptian Army Officers in this period wore light-blue shell jackets, and breaches with gold French epaulettes, and cuff chevrons with sleeve-length trefoil work. By 1885, the blue Infantry tunic had been adopted, with white collar and pointed cuffs, and was distinguished with blue (Infantry used white) shoulder boards[175]. After 1898, they likely used a blue flash on their Fez puggaree, as well as a tall blue plume hackie[176]. The uniform of the Camel Corps was later described wearing a soft Tarbush: Fez with green tassel, with a khaki twill jibba: long loose collarless coat with a short vent opening, with green plastron, cuffs and shoulders. Khaki twill Arab pantaloons, cut very loose, drab serge putties, and Arab sandals made of hide completed the dress.

C.Flaherty

174   Unknown, 1883.
175   Unknown, 1885.
176   British General Staff, 1912.

CHAPTER 13: FIRST WORLD WAR AND NATIONALIST ARMY CAVALRY

Prior to the start of the First World War the major change in the Cavalry appearance was introduction, in 1913 and 1914, with a new head-covering called the Kabalak or 'Enveryiye' sun hat named after Enver Pasha[177]. A fabric covered wicker frame with a drop-down neck and face cover, with long fabric ears that could be wrapped around the wearers face. Alongside the 1909 field brown suits the Cavalry, like the rest of the Imperial Army, from 1915 onwards adopted emergency issue tunics that came in a range of fabrics including linen, twill and wool, in colours ranging from light-sand, olive, light-green and darker yellow hues. Rather than produced at the Imperial Military Uniforms Factory in Constantinople, uniforms were made in field supply bases by Artisan-Soldiers Companies. The major design change was adding a fly-front covering the buttons. Field tailoring was also central to supply of the Nationalist Army, in 1921 till 1922 with new uniforms.

Army Officers in the First World War, and later Nationalist Army continued to wear the Kalpak as a rank distinction from their Soldiers (who wore either Kabalak-Enveryiye or Bashlik). The Greek-Turkish War era saw introduction of a new uniform style for Cavalry Officers and Soldiers, with issue of a peakless kepi/pill box hat with a thin leather chinstrap, covered in black oilcloth with a cast brass star and crescent badge on the front[178]. The origin of this cap was the 1916 replacement of the Fez, in the Imperial Navy for wear by its Sea Soldiers. In 1916, Navy Officer's also received a peakless low shako version that became the headgear for the Turkish Army in the 1920s.

By 1922, Nationalist Army Officers' Kalpak tended to appear larger and flatter at the top front, with the corners flaring-out, than the older model cylindrical versions. This style of hat, with a soft fabric dome was the same style worn in the Russian Army at the time, namely the Circassian lambswool cap. Cavalry also wore a cylindrical cloth hat with a broad folded brim issued to all the Army.

The typical mass issued tunic in 1922 was greenish-khaki wool with a low fall-down collar with plain cuffs, with five plain buttons down the front. It was provided with breast pockets, and sometimes larger hip pockets on the front of the low skirt. Commonly, a jacket version was worn with suit lapels (copied from British uniforms), and was worn with a black shirt and possibly tie, by some Cavalry units, but by mostly the Officers. British Officers'-style 'Sam Browne' belts and cross straps captured during the First World War, and later made in Turkey was a popular option for most ex-Imperial Army Officers. Riding breeches, long boots, shoes and leather leggings – all introduced into the Imperial Army in 1909 remained popular items of wear in the early 1920s Nationalist Army. By the end of the First World War, the Sultan Mehmed V Leibgarde-Kavallerie-Regiment – Ertogrul had changed its uniform. The 300-strong Sultan's Carriage Escort Guard were said to be well mounted on black horses wearing light blue dress uniforms, that had taken on the appearance of German Hussars. Wearing a Busby, and light blue Hussar jacket, and breeches decorated with gold-yellow cords. The Officers and Soldiers wore the Aides-de-Camp to the Sultan uniform insignia on their collars and incorporated into their cuff rank insignia.

---

177   British General Staff, 1995.
178   Jowett, 2015.

By 1922, Nationalist Army Cavalry had developed into an elite force[179]. During the latter stages of fighting in Asia Minor a number of Lancer units emerged unofficially amongst the Nationalist Cavalry, and several Lancer Regiments were in service by the end of the Greek-Turkish War. Whereas weapons remained ex-Imperial Army issue, black over red pennants were used rather than the plain red swallowtail.

▼ **A selection of Turkish Cavalry uniforms over the First World War: Officer, Lancer, and Dragoon.**

---

179   Jowett, 2015.

▼ A selection of Turkish Cavalry uniforms during the Greek-Turkish War (1919 till 1922): Lancer; Sultan's Carriage Escort Guard Officer, showing collar and Aides-de-Camp to the Sultan cuff insignia details; and, Cavalry Officer.

CHAPTER 14: CAMEL RAIDERS

Informally called the Camel Corps, initially three Battalions were identified in the Imperial Army in the First World War[180]. A Camel Mounted Unit was founded for the Canal Expedition, under the 10th Infantry Division, in 1914. Five additional Transport Camel Battalions, and several Independent Camel Companies were also organized. The 68th Infantry Regiment had a Camel Company in Mahdes. In Serapyum, there was a Camel Company with the 25th Division. In Elaris, there was a Volunteer Camel Company. On 9 June, 1915 the 4th Camel Regiment was forwarded to the Iraq front. On 22 July, till 25 August, 1915 the 2nd Camel Regiment was organized and sent to Iraq. From 15 June, till 15 July, 1915 a new Camel Regiment was established in Damascus. In January 1916, in Birussebi a Camel Company, under the 3rd Division was designated as Akinci: Raiders (Irregular Boarder Cavalry Corps that existed during the 16th Century). Following 1916, one of the Camel Raiders Companies became a 4th Army Headquarters Protection Unit and wore the sleeve patch (based on the Imperial Army's Stabsflaggen). This unit remained part of its parent formation, the 1st Camel Regiment, which was sent to the Hejaz Corps. The Regiment had three Camel Companies and a Machine Gun Company. There was also a second Camel Regiment stationed in Medina.

Camel Raiders Officers and Soldiers wore a distinctive field brown, green or sand coloured Zouave-styled jacket over a pull-over collared jersey[181]. Other troops wore a collarless Zouave-styled vest, that buttoned up at the shoulder seam, and sides, under the right or left arm[182]. This was commonly worn with a scarf, or neck wrap. A waist wrap completed the dress. Officers wore shoulder cords on the Zouave jackets. Facings were silver-grey, indicating the Cavalry; however, these may have been Mounted Infantry with dark grey-green facings – as photographs also show regular Army uniforms being worn. Officers wore the Kalpak, or the Keffiyeh along with the other Soldiers distinguished with a brass crescent badge (attached to the Agal when the Keffiyeh was worn). Keffiyeh headgear worn were a variety of tribal, family and individually coloured patterns, typically used in this period throughout the Middle East. Local Arab mounted equipment and gear was used[183].

▶ A Camel Raider Soldier (1916), showing the Agal and crescent badge details.

▶ This cast brass crescent headgear badge is 4 centimetres across and was traditionally used in the Imperial Army to indicate Auxiliary Soldiers, as well as troops with a special distinction. Such as the Camel Raiders.

---

180   British General Staff, 1995.
181   Orses, 2007.
182   Australian War Memorial.
183   American Colony of Jerusalem, 1915.

▼ A Camel Raiders Officer, and Officer from the 4th Army Headquarters Protection Unit (Camel Raiders Company, 1st Camel Regiment), with Army Stabsflaggen arm patch details.

C.Flaherty

CHAPTER 15: CAVALRY EQUIPMENT

Brown leather equipment is also shown as black. It is possible Turkish leather equipment like belts, sling straps and boots, horse harness and saddles were issued untreated brown and these progressively darkened through polishing and greasing. From 1879, Cavalry Junior Officers, and Nefer: Private Soldiers were equipped with a narrow leather belt with a steel open roll-buckle. It was not more than one inch wide and several buckle prong holes were visible along the belt. The belt supported a rear positioned ammunition wallet, which was supported by an additional narrow leather cross strap over the right shoulder. Another narrow leather cross strap with a roll-buckle (several buckle prong holes were also visible along the belt), and spring hooks fitted to either end, passed over the left shoulder, and went through a securing loop on the inside of the belt, at the side of the waist. The sword was slung from its scabbard rings. The alternative arrangement was the scabbard ring carry straps slings with spring hooks, and a carry-hook attached to a webbing belt worn under the tunic which had a double 'D-ring' attached along the lower edge. Officer's versions of the sword sling/cross strap were covered with gilt tape. The Ertugrul and 1st Lancers Regiments Officers had silver tape covered sword sling/cross straps. Fron the 1870s, the revolver pistol wallet was slung on the belt by Officers.

BELTS AND BUCKLES

Dragoons are often depicted wearing the Infantry Nefer: Private Soldiers' equipment waist belt[184]. Turkish Imperial and Egyptian Armies used the same equipment waist belt, and square brass plate buckle, displaying a crescent badge. The buckle was based on the French le Ceinturon Model 1873. The Turkish version was smaller to fit a 52 millimetres wide belt, designed to fit German 1874 Patronentasche fur Infantry: cartridge pouches used in the Imperial Army prior to 1908[185].

▼ Left: Turkish buckle were cast brass and based on French 19th Century models. Only the crescent was used by the Imperial Army up till 1908. Right: A 1909 Turkish belt buckle based on the German Army version used at the time. Asakr-i Shahaneh: Imperial Army is written in Ottoman-Turkish script within the crescent.

---

184   Askeri Muze, 1986.
185   Kurk, 2000.

GERMAN MAUSER CARTRIDGE POUCH

The major change in the appearance of the Cavalry after 1909, was the adoption of brown leather German-styled belts with Imperial Army buckle plates, and special modified Model 1909 German made Mauser three-pocket cartridge pouches. German made Mauser three-pocket cartridge pouches were cut down to two pockets, to accommodate the 30 rounds allocation for the Light Cavalry:

> "Light Cavalry Regiments carry thirty rounds of ammunition only, in two small pouches on the waist belt, three clips in each pouch. The remainder carry sixty rounds per man, in a canvas bag slung so as to fit close under the left arm, or in a waist bandolier."[186]

A 1917 photograph of Turkish Cavalry shows the modified Mauser pouches pushed around-back of the wearer's waist[187], like the previous rear positioned ammunition wallet.

▼ A Turkish modified German made Mauser pouch for the Light Cavalry.

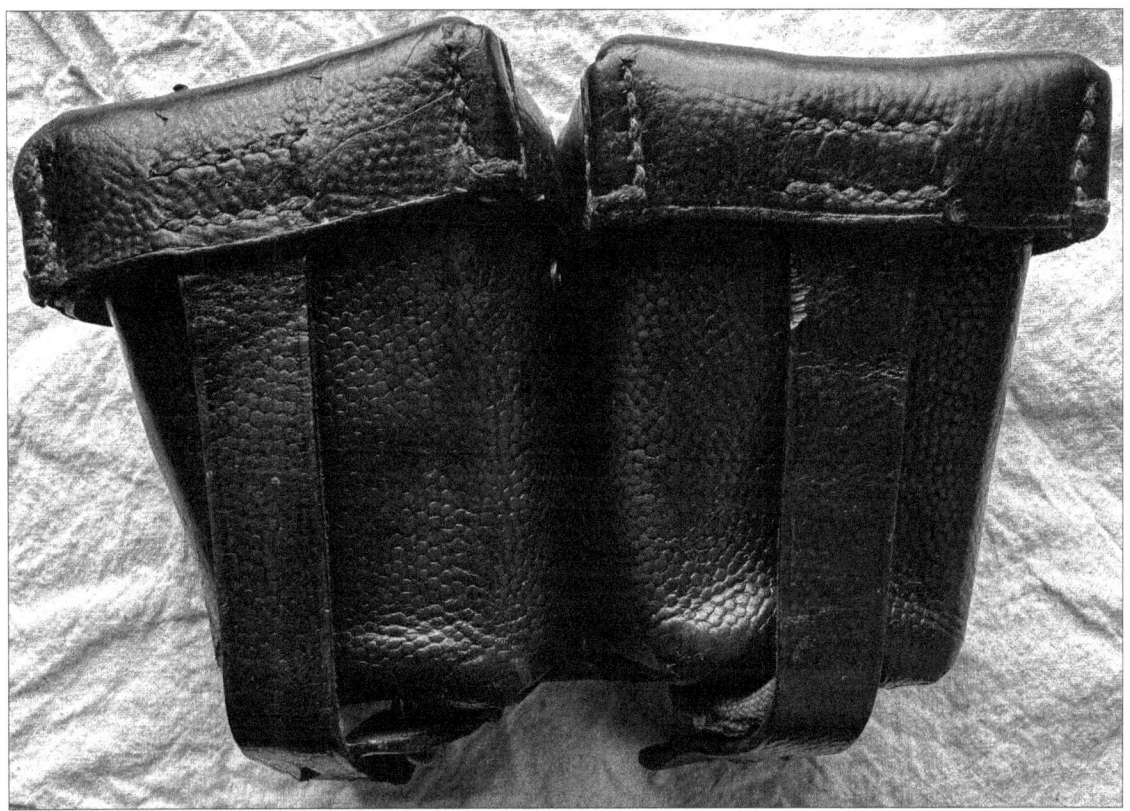

CAVALRY DRESS-UNIFORM CARTRIDGE BOXES

Cavalry continued to use the same cross-belt slung cartridge box from the 1861 era. The square pouch had sides faced with brass plates, with rings mounted, for the sling strap to hook onto. The square ended front flap was edged with a brass stripe, and the flap displayed an upwards facing crescent badge. The front end of the sling strap had a square, or sometimes heart-shaped plate with a crescent, or star and crescent badge. Behind this a metal arrow lock-pick on a chain could be inserted. The arrow lock-pick chain was connected to a crescent badge mounted further up.

---

186   British General Staff, 1995.
187   German Official Photographer, 1917.

▼ Officers' gold tape covered waist belt, and spring-hook design for attaching the scabbard ring, and cross-belt for the cartridge box. A Soldier's version of the cross-belt showing the arrow lock-pick on a chain, and plate details, and the cartridge box.

C.Flaherty

IMPERIAL ARMY CAVALRY LANCE

The Ertugrul Cavalry Regiment was equipped with lances, like the first Regiment in each of the Cavalry Divisions[188]. The other Regiments were armed with carbines. All Cavalry were sword armed. The Lancers used a French model lance. The pennant was plain red with a swallow tail with three attachment tapes[189]. A sleeved version was also likely in use. Some versions may have displayed a white star and crescent. The French lance was used till the Imperial Army Cavalry adopted in 1909 the German Army's steel shafted version - this was the German 1893 lance which was 10 feet, and 5 inches in length. A First World War photograph proports to show Arab Tribal Cavalry unit (reactivated former Hamidiye Cavalry), using lances/spears with long bamboo shafts, stated to be:

---

188 Askeri Muze, 1986.
189 Zonaro, 1901.

"military issue heavy lances"[190]. The 'heavy lances' are actually Arab Az-Zagayah: long hunting and fishing spear being used as a weapon, this had a long spear head, with a tasselled base[191][192].

▶ Turkish Cavalry stirrup and lance bucket, based on an 1895 illustration of the 1st Regiment of Lancers[193].

CAVALRY SWORD, SWORD KNOT AND PORTAPEE

The Imperial Army Cavalry sword (a), was used by the Cavalry Kolagasi: Adjutant-Major to the Nefer: Private Soldier[194]. It was a German-styled steel sabre with a 'P-guard' with sharkskin and wire handle and plain langet shield, with steel scabbard and rings. Nefer were distinguished by a French black leather sword knot, that ended with leather tassels. It was tied to the guard. Officers were also known to use other sword designs - a pre-First World War Turkish Cavalry Officer's sword[195], with a brass basket guard, and star and crescent shield, and black steel scabbard fitted with a 'L' shaped frog-button (b), with portapee (gold acorn and black cord for a Lower Grade Officer). The Ertugrul and 1st Lancers Regiments Officers' sabre (c), had a plain brass 'D-guard' with plain backstrap, and with a sharkskin and wire handle, steel scabbard and rings and drag, with silver portapee[196]. It was carried by the wearer using a sling/cross strap. The Cavalry Colonel to Regimental commander's sabre (d), plain brass 'D-guard' with leaf backstrap, sharkskin and wire handle, and langet shield displaying a star and crescent badge, with steel scabbard and rings and heavy drag, and with a gold portapee[197]. The design of the under-webbing belt with sword ring sling and carry-hook, and spring hook are shown[198].

◀ A First World Wartime Turkish Cavalry Soldier using a traditional Arab Az-Zagayah: long hunting and fishing spear, as a lance. Mounted on a long bamboo pole - more than 12 to 14 feet long, a long iron spear head, with a tasselled base was fitted.

THE 1909 SWORD

In 1909, orders were placed with German sword makers for a new standard Cavalry sabre. A total of 10,000 swords were likely delivered prior to 1914, to fully re-equip the Regular Cavalry. The 1909 Contract Swords were made by Solingen, or Carl Eickhorn. These had a full sheet steel bowl guard with turned edges, pierced with a five-point star and crescent badge. The 1909 sword had dark-brown checkered composite fibre/bakelite grips, was held to the tang by

---

190	Uyar, 2009.
191	Valfrio, 1856.
192	American Colony of Jerusalem, 1914.
193	Knotel, 1895.
194	Askeri Muze, 1986.
195	Private Collection.
196	Askeri Muze, 1986.
197	Askeri Muze, 1986.
198	Orses, 2007.

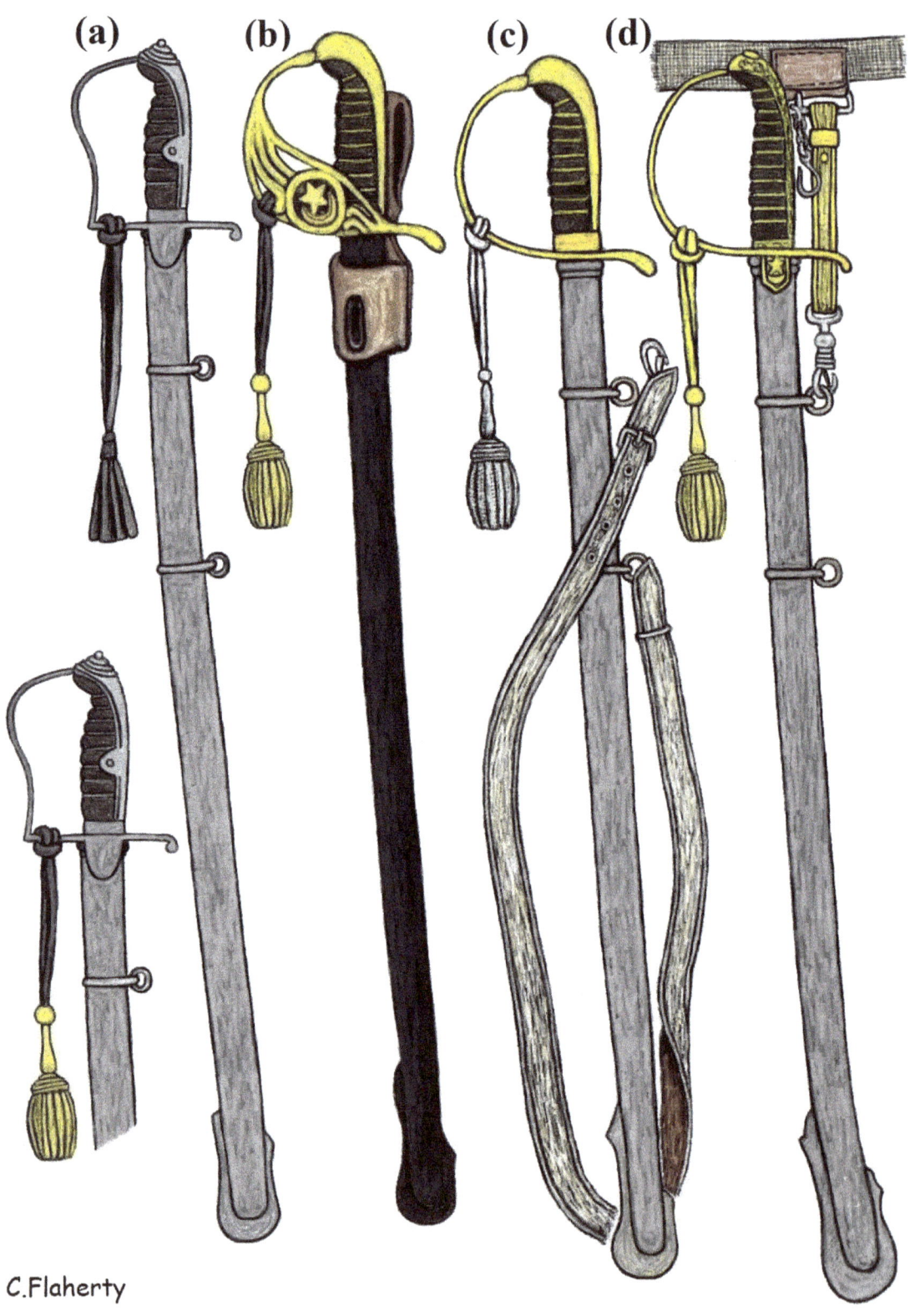

two rivets, and had a thumb groove to the top. The 1909 sword had a curved pipe backed blade, that was single edged, with a double edge spear point. The new sword was 33 to 34 inches in length, and including the guard equalled 39 inches overall. The all steel scabbard had a single (side) fixed strap ring on a band with a square loop at the back, and was designed to be carried strapped to the saddle[199]. Some versions are fitted with two (each side) fixed strap rings, on each side of the mouth, or a bronze 'L' shaped frog-button (identical to the 'D' Guard officers' short sword that came into use after 1909). A Brown canvas and leather cover, with a leather reinforced chape was provided for the scabbards, along with a separate brown canvas cover for the sword guard[200].

▶ The 1909 Contract Sword grip and guard with a pre-1908 sword knot. A 1909 Turkish large belt frog used by Infantry Officers to carry their short swords, and by the Cavalry for their sabre. A Turkish Cavalry sword carry wallet that strapped to the saddle.

BROWN LEATHER CHEST WALLET

An 1896 illustration shows a brown leather chest wallet positioned lengthwise under the crossing shoulder straps of Soldiers in the Ertugrul Regiment[201]. This same item appears in an 1893 photograph for the same Regiment[202]. This was a special dispatches carrying wallet.

HORSE EQUIPMENT

Cavalry saddlery was officially described as: "[the] Hungarian pattern saddle, with blue saddle cloth edged with regimental colour, and two leather wallets."[203] The schabracke is illustrated with rounded front and back ends[204]. It is blue with a wide bottle-green border (for the 4th Cavalry). A colourised

---

199	British General Staff, 1995.
200	Australian War Memorial.
201	Unknown, 1896.
202	Freres, 1893.
203	British General Staff, 1995.
204	Perboyre, 1910.

postcard from the period shows a Musician's schabracke, which was in contrasting red with gold borders[205]. An 1895 illustration shows a blue schabracke with a broad red border, with a second inner line of red tape, separated by a thin highlight of dark blue cloth showing[206]. No crescent badge can be seen displayed on the back ends. It was also provided with a large opening on the right-side to allow a rifle to pass-through, into a bucket. The rifle and bucket rested over the rider's right thigh, with the shoulder stock accessible to be pulled-out and used. An 1893 photograph of the Ertugrul Regiment Soldier shows the schabracke was more rigid, cut higher, with a front rounded end, and pointed back end[207]. A large cloth angled sideways facing crescent was added to the rear pointed end. A special wet weather oilskin cover for the schabracke is shown being used. An 1897 illustration shows a blue square blanket schabracke with a broad bottle-green border for the 4th Cavalry, including a bottle-green crescent badge displayed in the rear corner[208]. This same arrangement is also seen in an 1896 illustration[209]. Another 1895 illustration shows a short, pointed blue blanket schabracke with a broad red border (for the Line Cavalry), that disappears under the saddle[210]. A red crescent badge is displayed in the rear corner. By the start of the First World War the schabracke was replaced with a folded blanket under the saddle[211], this was possibly grey or white with two blue side stripes[212].

Turkish Cavalry saddle wallets came in two types slung over the front of the brown leather riding saddle on either side. The older type was a large oblong rounded brown leather bag with a rounded covering flap secured with a long leather tab. The newer type was more rectangular with formed sides, and had a cross strap over the face of the bag that secured the cover flap tab. The Ertugrul Cavalry attached a green parade cover (like the rest of the schabracke) over the saddle bags, with a thick red wide tape edge (silver for Officers), and a red crescent (silver for Officers) displayed in the middle[213]. The Sanjakdar: Standard Bearer Officer's saddle bag covers had a red border with a silver crescent as a special distinction. Senior Officers, used a saddle brace of pistol holsters with brass tubes, carrying ornate Turkish pistols, that were covered by a round ended (sometimes pointed) cloth cover, with a wide gilt or silver tape border.

A grey blanket or coat is usually depicted rolled and strapped to the back of the saddle, where a portemanteau valise is usually placed. The portemanteau was blue cloth displaying a red end ring, with an inner blue circular patch. A smaller grey cloth covered portemanteau with a closed ends secured with a drawstring was also used by the 1890s.

205	Private Collection.	
206	Knotel, 1895.	
207	Freres, 1893.	
208	**Demoulin, 1897.**	
209	Unknown, 1896.	
210	Knotel, 1895.	
211	German Official Photographer, 1917.	
212	Unknown.	
213	Zonaro, 1901.	

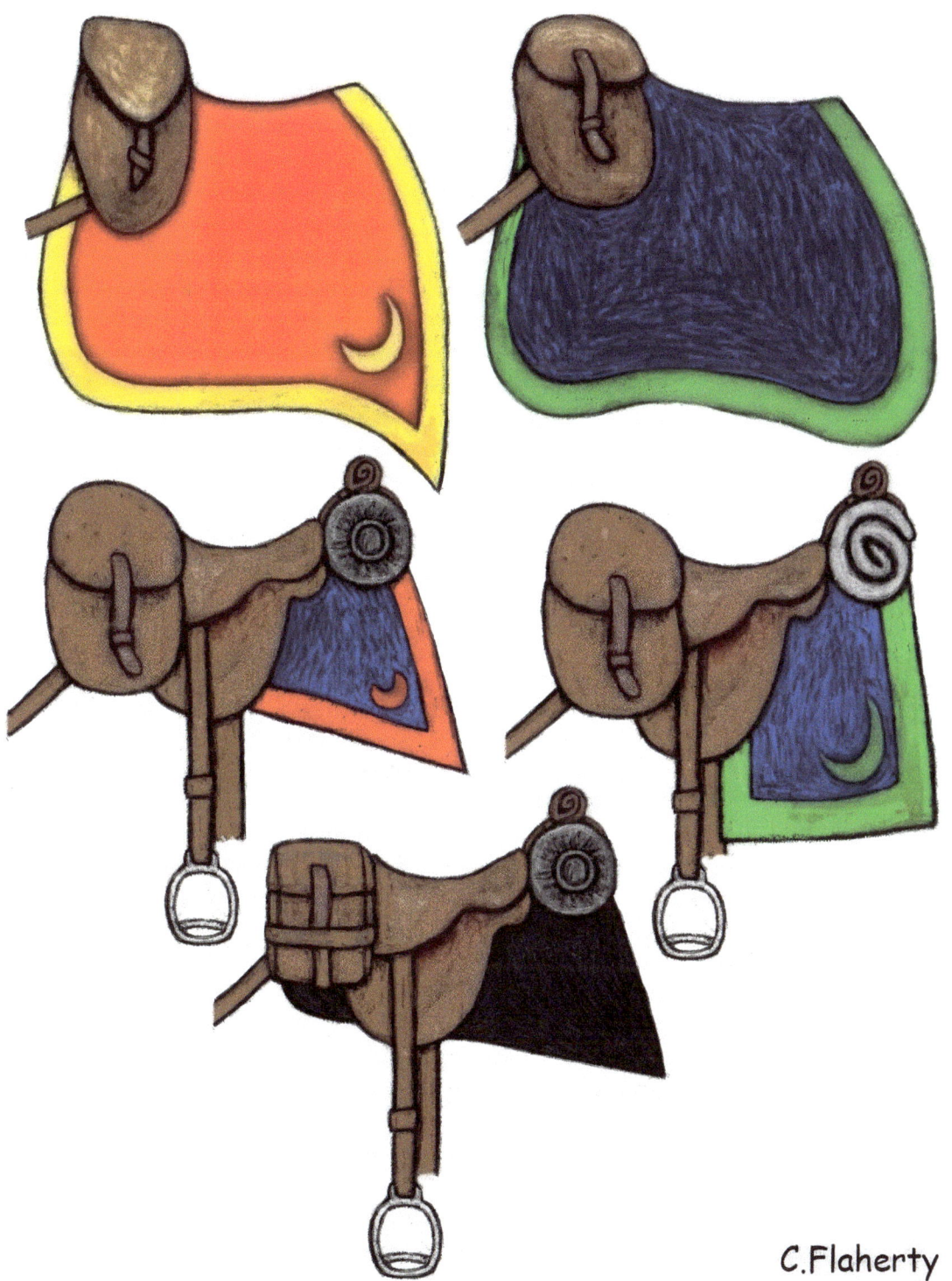

Horse schabracke for a 4th Cavalry Regiment Musician; horse schabracke for the 4th Cavalry Regiment (1895); Line Regiment horse schabracke; 4th Cavalry Regiment horse's square blanket schabracke (1896); and, Ertugrul Regiment's special wet weather oilskin cover for the schabracke, with grey cloth covered portemanteau.

REFERENCES

- American Colony of Jerusalem. 1914 Arab Bedoin Warrior Carrying Long Hunting Az-Zagayah. Photograph. Library of Congress. Eric, G. Matson, E. Collection Call Number: LC-M36-612.
- American Colony of Jerusalem. 1915 The Camel Corps at Beersheba. Photograph. Library of Congress. Eric, G. Matson, E. Collection Call Number: LC-DIG-ppmsca-13709-00037.
- American Colony of Jerusalem. 1917 Izzat [Izzet] Pasha and Jamal [Cemal] Pasha. Photograph. Library of Congress. Eric, G. Matson, E. Collection Call Number: LC-DIG-ppmsca-13709-00191.
- Annuaire Oriental Du Commerce. 1891 De L'Industrie, De L'Administration Et De La Magistrature. Constantinople. Bibliotheque Nationale de France.
- Army and Navy Gazette. 1900 Types of the Egyptian Army. Illustration. Number 147 (3 March).
- Army and Navy. 1914 The Sultan's Army: Turkish Troops and German Methods (5 December).
- Askeri Muze [National Army Military Museum, Istanbul]. 1986 Osmanli Askeri Teskilat ve Kiyafetleri [Ottoman Military Organization and Uniforms]: 1876-1908. Askeri Muze ve Kultur Sitesti Komutanligi Yayinlari.
- Askeri Muze [National Army Military Museum, Istanbul]. 1917 Special Award Banner of the 79th Infantry Regiment Who Defended Gaza, Palestine. Collection Item.
- Askeri Muze [National Army Military Museum, Istanbul]. Light Blue Ottoman Dragoons' Dolman-Jacket. Collection Item.
- Auctions Imperial [Antique Arms & Armor]. 2012 A Rare Suit of Sudanese Armor. Lot: 244.
- Australian War Memorial. Turkish Cavalry Trooper's Sword, with Canvas Covered Guard and Covered Scabbard. Collection Accession Number: REL/16346.
- Australian War Memorial. 1916 Portrait of a Turkish Prisoner, One of a Number Who Were Captured by the Anzac Mounted Division, Magdhaba on 23 December, 1916. Photograph. Collection Number: J00990.
- Australian War Memorial. 1918 Regimental Standard the 46th Turkish Infantry Regiment Captured Near Damascus. Collection Accession Number: RELAWM04772.
- Bartlett, E.A. 1897 The Battlefields of Thessaly: With Personal Experiences in Turkey and Greece. John Murray, London.
- Beamont, W. 1856 A Diary of a Journey to the East, in the Autumn of 1854. London: Longman, Brown, Green, and Longman.
- Boustead, J.E.H. 1934 The Camel Corps of the Sudan Defence Force. Royal United Services Institution Journal. Volume 79. Issue 515.
- Britannica [Encyclopædia]. 2025 Bashi-Bazouk.
- British General Staff. 1912 Handbook of the Egyptian Army. London.
- British General Staff. 1995 [The] 1916 Handbook of the Turkish Army. Battery Press. Nashville.
- Callwell, C.E. 1892 Handbook of the Turkish Army. London: Harrison and Sons, St. Martin's Lane (HMSO).
- Charton, M.E. 1840 Forces Militaires de Mehemet-Ali. Uniformes et Insignnes des Differents Corps de l'Armee Egyptienne. Le Magasin Pittoresque. Paris.
- Cox, M. Lenton, J. 1997 Crimean War Basics: Organisation and Uniforms: Russia and Turkey. Partizan Press.

- Critical Past. Sultan Mehmed V Gets Off a Carriage in Turkey before World War I. Fim Clip: 65675051116.
- Deroy, I. 1855 Debarquement de l'Armee Turque e Eupatoria: Commandee par Omer Pasha. Illustration. Anne S.K. Brown Military Collection. BDR: 233574.
- Dodd, G. 1856 Pictorial History of the Russian War, 1854-56. Edinburgh and London: W.R. Chambers.
- Donne, B.D.A. 1890 Major General Grenfel Watching the Advance of the 9th and 10th Sudanese Battalions of the Egyptian Army Against the Mahdists at Toski, 1889. Painting. National Army Museum [United Kingdom]. Collection National Accession Number: 1979-07-111-6.
- Demoulin, V. Chartier, H. 1897 [-1904]. Turquie (Armes, Drapeaux, Armee). Nouveau Larousse Illustre [New Larousse Illustrated French Language Encyclopedia].
- Druck [der], K.K. 1905 Die Turkische Armee. Druck der K.K. Hof- und Staatsdruckerei. Wien.
- Drury, I. 2012 The Russo-Turkish War 1877. Osprey Publishing.
- Dunn, J.P. 2013 Khedive Ismail's Army. Taylor & Francis Ltd.
- Ellens, J.H. 2013 Winning Revolutions: The Psychosocial Dynamics of Revolts for Freedom, Fairness, and Rights. ABC-CLIO.
- Falls, C. Becke, A.F. (Maps) 1930 Military Operations Egypt & Palestine from June 1917 to the End of the War. Official History of the Great War. Volume 2. London: HM Stationery Office.
- Freres, A. 1893 [-1880] The Standard Bearer and Guards of the Second Cavalry Regiment of the Imperial Guard. Photograph. Library of Congress: Abdul Hamid II Collection. LOT 9539. Number 36 [Item].
- Freres, A. 1893 [-1880] The Standard Bearer and Guards of the First Regiment of Lancers of the Imperial Guard. Photograph. Library of Congress: Abdul Hamid II Collection. LOT 9539. Number 20 [Item].
- Freres, A. 1893 [-1880] Standard Bearer and Guards of the Ertugrul Cavalry Regiment of the Imperial Guard. Photograph. Library of Congress: Abdul Hamid II Collection. LOT 9539. Number 8 [Item].
- Freres, A. 1893 [-1880] The Standard Bearer of the First Mobile Artillery Bodyguard Brigade. Photograph. Library of Congress: Abdul Hamid II Collection. LOT 11905. Number 4 [Item].
- Freres, A. 1893 [-1880] Ertugrul Cavalry Regiment of the Imperial Guard. Photograph. Library of Congress: Abdul Hamid II Collection. LOT 9539. Number 2 [Item].
- Freres, A. 1893 [-1880] Naim Bey, Lieutenant Colonel in the Ertugrul Cavalry Regiment of the Imperial Guard. Photograph. Library of Congress: Abdul Hamid II Collection. LOT 9539. Number 10 [Item].
- Freres, A. 1893 [-1880] Soldier of the Ertugrul Cavalry Regiment of the Imperial Guard. Photograph. Library of Congress: Abdul Hamid II Collection. LOT 9539. Number 15 [Item].
- German Official Photographer. 1917 A Unit of Turkish Cavalry Riding Through a Village. Photograph. Imperial War Museum Catalogue Number: Q86403.
- German Official Photographer. 1917 Kaiser Wilhelm II driving in a State Carriage with Sultan Mehmed V, with Cavalry Escort, on His Arrival at Constantinople, 15 October 1917. Photograph. Imperial War Museum Catalogue Number: Q79580.
- German Official Photographer. 1917 Cemal Pasha at His Headquarters. Photograph. Imperial War Museum Catalogue Number: Q45339.
- German Official Photographer. 1917 An Unit of Turkish Cavalry Crossing the River Jordan. Photograph. Imperial War Museum Catalogue Number: Q86393.

- Giles, G.D. 1899 After the Battle. The Emir Mahmud Brought Prisoner to Herbert Kitchener, Atbara, 8 April 1898. Painting. National Army Museum [United Kingdom]. Collection National Accession Number: 1978-08-29-1.
- Goupil-Fesquet, F.A.A. 1843 Cavalerie Egyptienne Giseh. Coloured Print.
- Graphic [The]: An Illustrated Weekly Newspaper. 1904 British Officers in the Ottoman Gendarmerie. Number 1,804. Volume LXIX. Saturday (25 June).
- Graphic [The]: An Illustrated Weekly Newspaper. 1883. Number 730. Volume XXVIII. Saturday (24 November).
- Graves, R.W. 1933 British Gendarmerie Officers in Macedonia, 1907. Storm Centres of the Near East. Hutchinson, London.
- Greene, F.D. 1895 The Armenian Crisis in Turkey: the Massacre of 1894, its Antecedents and Significance. The Knickerbocker Press. Photograph. British Library Collection. Accession Number: HMNTS 9055.aaa.40.
- Hacisalihoglu, M. 2007 Standard Presentation to Newly Founded Regiment, in 1844 by Sultan Abdulmecid. Illustration. Osmanli Imparatorlugu'nda Zorunlu Askerlik Sistemine Gecis Ordu-Millet Dusuncesi [The Transition to Compulsory Military Service in the Ottoman Empire]. Toplumsal Tarih. Number 164 (August).
- Imperial War Museum. Turkish Army's Third Cavalry Division Pennant. Collection on Display. Item Display Number 27.
- Johnson, D. 1972 The Egyptian Army 1880-1900: Uniforms, Flags, and Numbers. Savage and Soldier Magazine. Volume VIII. Number 1.
- Johnson, D. 1972 Bashi-Bazouks in the Sudan. Savage and Soldier Magazine. Volume XVII. Number 4 (October-December).
- Johnson, D. 1969 The Egyptian Camel Corps 1883-1885. Savage and Soldier. Volume V. Number 1-2 (June).
- Jowett, P. 2015 Armies of the Greek-Turkish War 1919–22. Osprey Publishing. Men-at-Arms, 501.
- Knotel, R. 1897 Die Turkische Armee und Marine. Rathenow Max Babenzien.
- Knotel, R. 1895 Garde Ulanen-Regiment (Parade). Uniformenkunde - Turkei.
- Knotel, R. 1895 Linien-Kavallerie. Uniformenkunde - Turkei.
- Kodaman, B. 2011 The Hamidiye Light Cavalry Regiments: Abdul Hamid II and the Eastern Anatolian Tribes. Yavuz, H. Sluglett, P. (Editors) War and Diplomacy: the Russo-Turkish War of 1877-1878 and the Treaty of Berlin. Salt Lake City: the University of Utah Press.
- Kurk, A.A. 2000 Patronetaschen Patrogengurtel Und Banduliere 1850-1950. KRUK.
- Le Petit Journal. 1895 Armee Ottomane. Riza-Bey - Commandant de Cavalerie, Aide-de-Camp de S.M.I. le Sultan. Cover Illustration (24 November).
- Lekegian, G. 1902 Major-General Lord Kitchener of Khartoum. Coloured Photograph. Cairo.
- London Illustrated News. 1882. Cuirassier of the Guard. Illustration.
- Lutsky, V.B. 1969 Modern History of the Arab Countries. Progress Publishers. Moscow.
- Lynch, H.F.B. 1901 Armenia, Travels and Studies. Volume 2. Longmas, Green, and Company.
- Mango, A. 1999 Ataturk. John Murray.
- Montbard, G. 1882 The Crisis in Egypt: Types of Soldiers in the Egyptian Army. London Illustrated News. Number 2218. Volume IXXX. Saturday (3 June).
- National Army Museum. 1898 Kulah Khud, Persian Style Helmet. Collection National Accession Number: 1963-10-186-1.

- National Military Museum. Khedive Bodyguard Squadron of Lancers Uniform. Collection on Display. Cairo Citadel.
- Ollier, E. 1890 Illustrated History of the Russo-Turkish War. Volume 1. London.
- Orses, T. Ozcelik, N. 2007 Dunya Savasi'nda Turk Askeri Kiyafetleri 1914-1918 [The WW1 Turkish Military]. Militarmuseum, Istanbul.
- Perboyre, P-E. 1910 Types Militaires Turcs. Illustration.
- Peri, O. 2005 Ottoman Symbolism in British-Occupied Egypt, 1882-1909. Middle Eastern Studies. Volume 41. Number 1 (January).
- Private Collection. Turkish Cavalry Musician. Colourised Postcard. Late 19th Century.
- Private Collection. Turkish Cavalry Officer's Sword with Cast Brass Guard, and Star and Cresent Badge.
- Private Collection [C.N. Initials]. 1908 Full Dress Uniform of a Major in the 1st Lancers Regiment. Photograph.
- Private Collection [C.N. Initials]. 1914 A Type of Cavalryman of the Turkish Army. Photograph.
- Pyhrr, S.W. 1989 European Armor from the Imperial Ottoman Arsenal. Metropolitan Museum Journal 24.
- Robinson, H.R. 1967 Oriental Armour [The Arms and Armour Series]. Walker & Company.
- Roubicek, M. 1978 Modern Ottoman Troops, 1797-1915: In Contemporary Pictures. Franciscan Printing Press.
- Royle, C. 1886 The Egyptian Campaigns, 1882 to 1885. Volume II. Hurst & Blackett.
- Ruhl, M. 1914 Die Armeen der Balkanstaaten: Turkei, Griechenland, Rumanien, Serbien, Bulgarien, Montenegro in Ihren Gegenwartigen Uniformierungen [The Armies of the Balkan States: Turkey, Greece, Romania, Serbia, Bulgaria, Montenegro in their Present Uniforms]. Leipzig.
- Ruhl, M. 1900 [Circa: Published From] Die Armeen der Balkan-Staaten. II. Turkei u. Griechenland [The Armies of the Balkans. Turkey and Greece: Volume 2]. Leipzig: Moritz Ruhl.
- Sakip Sabanci Museum. Fabric Panel From Ottoman Standard. Late 19th Century. Sabanci University Collection.
- Servet-i-Funun [The Wealth of Knowledge Magazine]. 1896 Les Officiers du Regiment Hamidie de la Cavalerie Formee des Carapapaks. Volume 8. Number 413. Alem Printing House Ahmet İhsan and Company, Constantinople.
- Servet-i-Funun [The Wealth of Knowledge Magazine]. 1891 Le Regiment de la Cavalerie Hamidie de Kiss a Ourfa. Volume 5. Number 115. Alem Printing House Ahmet Ihsan and Company, Constantinople.
- Sevket, M. [Mahmoud Chevket Pasha] 1907 L'Organization et les Uniformes de l'Armee Ottomanne. Premiere Partie.
- Turker, G.K. 2022 Osmanli Imparatorlgu Askeri Kiyafetleri [Military Clothing of the Ottoman Empire] 1826-1922. Hisart Canli Tarih Muzeesi Kultur Yayinian 2.
- Unknown. Reiter (Leibgarde des Sultans). Turkiches Heer, Book Illustration. Possibly Late 19th Century. Alamy. Image ID: 2EA6KBG.
- Unknown. 1850 [-1896] Leib-Regiment Ertegrul. Vinkhuijzen, H.J. [Collection]. New York Public Library [The]. Image ID: 435726.
- Unknown. 1880 [-1893] Interior of the Weapons Museum - Armory Museum of Ayairene (Church of St. Irene). Photograph. Library of Congress: Abdul Hamid II Collection. LOT 11910, Number 3 [Item].

- Unknown. 1883 Egyptian Guardia del Ministra Officer. Photograph. Private Collection.
- Unknown. 1883 [1898-1820]. Guardia del Ministra. Vinkhuijzen, H.J. [Collection]. New York Public Library [The]. Image ID: 1607001.
- Unknown. 1885 [1898-1820]. Kameelcorps der Egyptischen Armee. Vinkhuijzen, H.J. [Collection]. New York Public Library [The]. Image ID: 1607008.
- Unknown. 1890 Hamidiye Corps Miralai, and Aide-de-Camp to the Sultan. Photograph.
- Unknown. 1896 Erste Arcieren-Leibgarde; Trabanten-Leibgarde. Vinkhuijzen, H.J. [Collection]. New York Public Library [The]. Image ID: 91775.
- Unknown. 1896 [-1909] Turkei. Ulan.-Reg. Linien-Cavallerist. Leib-Cav.-Reg. "Ertogrul" Unteroffizier. Vinkhuijzen, H.J. [Collection]. New York Public Library [The]. Image ID: 435765.
- Unknown. 1898 [-1820] Egyptian Cavalry From the One Regiment Organised, Under Colonel Taylor of the 19th Hussars and Captain Kitchener. Vinkhuijzen, H.J. [Collection]. New York Public Library [The]. Image ID: 1607011.
- Unknown. 1901 Kurdish Hamidiye Officer. Photograph.
- Unknown. 1909 Two Officers from Sultan Mehmed V Mounted Bodyguard Troop. Photograph Number 24186.
- Uyar, M. Erickson, E.J. 2009 A Military History of the Ottomans. Greenwood.
- Valfrio. 1856 Arab Sentry of the Turkish Irregular Army. London Illustrated News (12 January).
- Varli, A.M. 1995 Osmanli-Rus ve Iran Savaslar'inda Kurtler [The Kurds in the Ottoman-Russian and Iranian Wars], 1801-1900. Ankara: SIPAN.
- War Office [The]. 2008 [The] 1915 Notes on the Turkish Army: With a Short Vocabulary of Turkish Words and Phrases. N & M Press.
- Zonaro, F. 1901 The Ertugrul Cavalry Regiment Crossing the Galata Bridge. National Palaces Collection Istanbul.

OTHER TITLES BY THE SAME AUTHOR

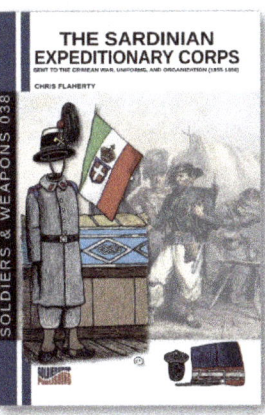

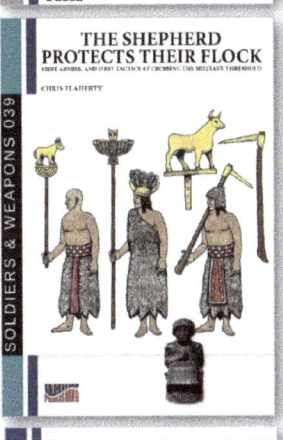

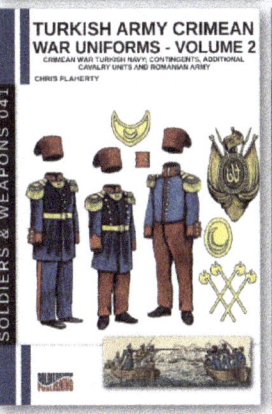

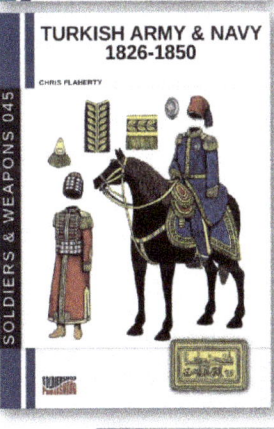

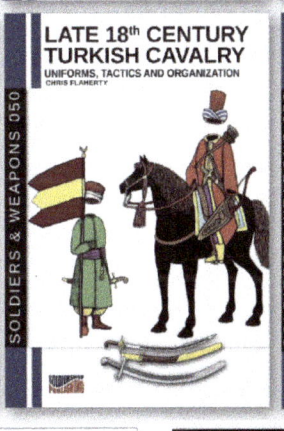
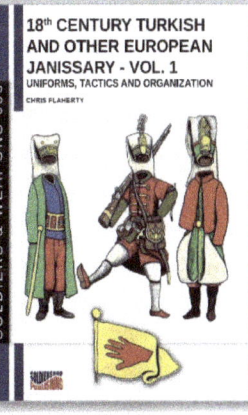
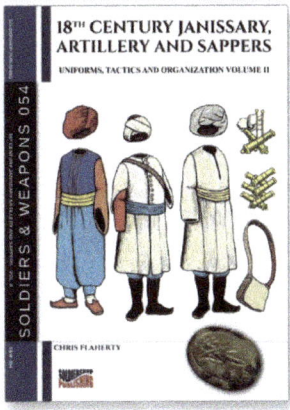
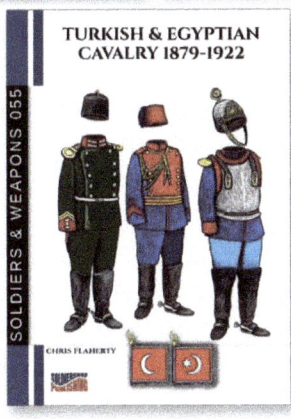
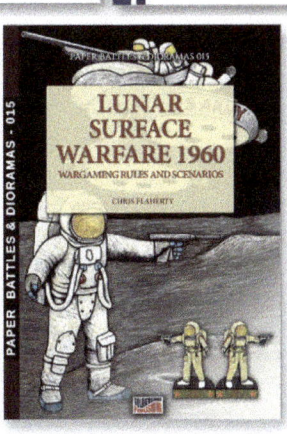

SOLDIERS & WEAPONS 055

www.ingramcontent.com/pod-product-compliance
Lightning Source LLC
LaVergne TN
LVHW070523070526
838199LV00072B/6686